Services

OTHER VOLUMES IN THE
Conservation of Human Resources Series

Services

THE NEW ECONOMY

Thomas M. Stanback, Jr.
Peter J. Bearse
Thierry J. Noyelle
Robert A. Karasek

Foreword by Eli Ginzberg

LandMark Studies
ALLANHELD, OSMUN Publishers

ALLANHELD, OSMUN & CO. PUBLISHERS, INC.

Published in the United States of America in 1981
by Allanheld, Osmun & Co. Publishers, Inc.
(A Division of Littlefield, Adams & Company)
81 Adams Drive, Totowa, New Jersey 07512

Library of Congress Cataloging in Publication Data
Main entry under title:

Services/The New Economy

   (Conservation of human resources series; 20)
   Bibliography: p.
   Includes index.
   1. Service industries — United States. 2. United
States — Economic conditions — 1971-   I. Stanback,
Thomas M. II. Series.
HD9981.5.S45   330.973'0927   81-10905
ISBN 0-916672-63-8   AACR2

81 82 83 84 / 10 9 8 7 6 5 4 3 2 1

Printed in the United States of America

Contents

Tables and Figures

Foreword

For the last decade and a half the Conservation of Human Resources Project, Columbia University, has been exploring the transformations that are taking place in the economy of the United States, primarily from the vantage of the growing importance of the not-for-profit sector that is so heavily engaged in the output of services. Its initial effort was *The Pluralistic Economy*, by Eli Ginzberg, Dale L. Hiestand, and Beatrice Reubens.* The intervening years have seen a number of related publications, the more important of which are included in the bibliography at the end of the present monograph.

My colleagues and I were drawn initially to the subject of the shift toward services because of our concern with understanding the changing dynamics of job creation. It was clear by the early 1960s that manufacturing was no longer the dominant source of job creation. If not manufacturing, what then? Our preliminary explorations pointed to the growing importance of government and nonprofit institutions as lead sectors, involving rapidly growing outputs in education, health, defense, community infrastructure, and research and development.

In subsequent inquiries our research efforts broadened to

*McGraw-Hill, 1965.

take account of the locational aspects of business activity and the feedback relations between the profit and the not-for-profit sectors, and to explore the quality of the jobs that were opening up rapidly as a result of the expansion of services.

Early in 1979 Citicorp — with Executive Vice President for Strategic Planning George Vojta in the lead and with the cooperation of the Economics Department (Mr. Lief Olson and associates) — made funds available to the Conservation of Human Resources to institute a multi-faceted exploration of the role of services in the U.S. economy. This effort included the following approaches: a series of dialogues with distinguished economists; a reassessment of the system of national accounts as it relates to services; case studies of selected corporations that have expanded into services; and a reevaluation of the state of the literature coupled with an attempt to advance the conceptualization of services. The current monograph represents the product of the last item on the research agenda.

Since the results of this effort are presented tersely and without recourse to jargon, there is little point to my providing a summary of the findings. Those who are interested in the subject should read the entire work. Rather I will call attention to a limited number of points that have impressed me as more or less new and important, and by singling them out I hope to encourage the reader to read the work and draw his or her own conclusions.

Now to the key points:

Economists for the most part have been quite muddled in their approach to services. They have concentrated largely on "consumer services" from beauty parlors to dry cleaning establishments, which represent the smallest of the six major subdivisions of services.

The strategic role of producer services in the contemporary economy both in terms of scale and growth has almost totally escaped notice. The authors estimate that producer services account for approximately 25 percent of GNP, which means that they account for more value added than all manufacturing. Moreover, they are the fastest growing sector of the economy.

The dominant role of producer services reflects in considerable measure the combined effects of the growth of markets, the growth of firms, the growth of income and product differentiation, and the changing role of technology. Large firms operating in national and international markets need the help of sizable, specialized staffs for planning and control, as well as for innovation, marketing, and other management functions that require more specialists both in-house and out-of-house.

It is incorrect to visualize the United States economy as turning its back on the production of goods and concentrating increasingly on the production of services. That, as the authors emphasize, is an oversimplification. Rather the nature of how production takes place is undergoing rapid change, with more and more dependence on the role of producer services.

Services, which in total account for almost seven out of every ten jobs, include jobs that are good, fair, and poor. The authors believe that employment in services is resulting in a bifurcation with more and more workers at the two extremes, holding either well-paid, prestigious jobs or poorly paid, unrewarding jobs with little security and few benefits. I am not yet convinced that there is such a clear-cut trend, much less that it will continue; but the authors' evidence is worth careful consideration, for if true it has ominous implications for a society in which the pursuit of equity is a leit-motif.

Conventional economic theory is shackled to static foundations with a narrow economic perspective, while economic development in advanced economies, which includes the growth of services, requires a dynamic approach where the framework is more inclusive and makes room for changes in societal institutions and values.

The authors make a strong case for a broadened and deepened approach to the study of economic change, but they would be the first to acknowledge that their sketch of the directions to follow is merely a sketch. But it is important to recognize that it was their fruitful and insightful inquiry into services that precipitated these larger concerns. If others agree and follow them up, this monograph on services — important in its own terms — will prove even more important by helping to break the bonds of the conventional framework for analysis, which is daily proving itself inadequate on many fronts, to illuminate the changing reality which is a U.S. economy in rapid transition. Services have produced a good vantage from which to address the larger and more important subject of where the U.S. economy is headed and how we may be able to direct it toward ends that contribute to the greater well-being of the individual and the security of the nation.

Eli Ginzberg, Director
Conservation of Human Resources
Columbia University
June 1981

Acknowledgments

As we complete this analysis of the role of services in the American economy in the late twentieth century, we find ourselves indebted to two distinctly different groups of individuals.

The first is those scholars who have preceded us and whose ideas and findings provided important insights to the significance of recent developments. Our acknowledgments are explicit in the numerous references to their work.

The second is those colleagues whose suggestions, criticisms, encouragements, or direct assistance have helped so much along the way. Our greatest debt by far is to Eli Ginzberg who, as director of the overall Citicorp study of services, continuously supplied the reassurance, sound counsel, and sense of excitement and purpose that were so important in preparing this manuscript. Our thanks go also to George Vojta for his continued support of this project and to Leif Olson, Peter Crawford, Jacqueline Brandwynne, Robert Lewis, and other members of Citicorp's Strategic Planning and Economic staffs who provided an essential element to the research environment by making themselves available as a forum for presenting and defending the tentative findings of our investigation on several occasions.

Finally we wish to thank our research assistant, Tom Wong, for his contribution in preparing the empirical material.

I. Introduction

The transformations at work within the American economy are at once dramatic and complex. Deeply implicated is the growth of service employment — from 55 percent to roughly two-thirds of all jobs during the period 1929– 1977. This growth has involved chiefly an expansion in the nonprofit services (health and education), in government and, what is not generally understood, in the producer services (finance, insurance, legal counseling, advertising, consulting or advertising).[1]

In large measure the expansion of these leading groups of service activities has resulted from a growing need for intermediate services and investment in human capital in an economy characterized by an increased sophistication in terms of *what* it produces and *how* it carries out production. To put this transformation into perspective, we estimate that 25 percent of the GNP originates today from the production of mostly intermediate producer services, as much as the share of the GNP resulting from the physical production of manufactured goods (see below). Such producer services are used for the most part in the production of goods (R&D, data processing, financing of inventories and purchases, etc.) or in getting the goods into the hands of the purchasers (marketing, advertising, financing of deliveries, etc.)

This view of the transformation differs sharply from that of others who have searched for an explanation of a tilting of the economy almost solely in terms of final outputs of services. In

addition, it has the advantage of reconciling the intuitive
notion of the growing importance of the services in our advanced economy with an essentially correct, popular vision
that ours is a society which remains very much goods-
oriented.

The Services: Four Misconceptions

In considerable measure the confusion that prevails regarding the nature of growth in services arises out of four misconceptions: the misconception of homogeneity, the misconception of limitations on scale economies, the misconception as to
the nature of certain service outputs, and the misconception
of spacelessness. Together these imperfect or inadequate
ways of looking at services have led to a tendency to misunder-
stand where growth in service employment has occurred and
to a simplistic view that the differential in growth rates in
service employment merely reflects a relatively low rate of
productivity improvement that characterizes all service activities when compared to the record for producers of goods
taken as a whole.

The Misconception of Homogeneity. It seems fair to say that the
tendency to think of services as a more or less homogeneous
group of activities is the result of writers, both within and
outside the ranks of economists, treating "services" as a "sector" of the economy (differentiated from another major sector, "goods") and reporting growth in output and employment for all services combined. Thus we have come to speak,
uncritically, of the rise of services and of the development of a
service economy, often called "the postindustrial society."

Even Victor Fuchs, in his seminal work on *The Service
Economy* (1968), tended to restrict the nature of the transformation by emphasizing almost exclusively the role of consumer and public sector services. Only minor significance was
assigned to changes in the composition of "intermediate" versus "final" demand, with the result that the role played by
some key intermediate services was largely overlooked. As
Edward Denison (1979) has observed: "The statement that
the service share of employment has risen from 50 percent to
60 percent creates the impression that barbershops and laun-

dries have replaced manufacturing as the mainstay of the economy and that the shift has been a general one."

In addition to this misconception regarding the homogeneity of service output there has been a tendency among certain sociologists and economists to misconstrue the nature of employment created by the services. The work of some of them may have lead to a belief that the transformation to a service economy is bringing about a generalized upgrading of work, as manifested by the growth of managerial, professional, and semiprofessional occupations. As our work will show, this portrayal of the changes in the occupational structure seriously overlooks some real and serious problems that arise at the other.end of the occupational spectrum.

In short, the carelessness with which we treat services extends beyond a mere tendency toward excessive aggregation in discussing growth and productivity trends. It leads to a failure to observe that different service activities are characterized by different rates of expansion, that they differ widely in the ways in which they utilize capital and human resources, and that their growth is propelled by different sets of social and economic forces.

The Misconception of Limitations in Scale Economies. A misconception that has long lingered is that service activities are severely limited by scale economies except in the areas of transportation, communications, utilities, and in some parts of the financial sector. Only in the past ten years has this notion been seriously called into question.

The major difficulty in examining limitations on scale in services arises out of the failure to distinguish between economies that relate to the size of individual establishments and those that relate to the entire firm. Unlike goods, services cannot be stockpiled and shipped; they must be delivered directly to the customer. This often means that the individual establishment is unable to serve more than a limited area.

Thus, limitations in market size rather than limitations in production economies seem to be more important in accounting for the relatively small scale of service establishments. Such constraints, however, need not limit size of firm where the firm operates on a multi-unit basis. The operation of a firm whether in goods or services requires the performance of a number of functions (which will be discussed in Chapter 3). At least some functions may be performed subject to significant economies of scale by having them performed centrally for a number of establishments. Thus we find that for a wide variety of branched and franchised service operations, functions such as accounting, finance, advertising, training, and general management are carried on outside the establishment that serves the public.

The extent to which scale economies are available within services is a matter which requires additional study, but it is clearly a misconception to think of service firms as uniformly restricted to small-scale operation.

Misconceptions and Problems in Measuring Output. Services by their very nature are difficult to measure. Intangible and rendered directly to the customer, they are less likely than goods to be standardized. The service often differs from customer to customer (viz. the services of the doctor, lawyer, accountant, or banker to his patients or clients) and is not readily defined in terms of either quality or quantity. Moreover, there is an interaction between customer and seller that affects both the quality of the service and the efficiency with which it is rendered (Fuchs 1980). If the borrower keeps accurate and complete records, the bank is likely to be able to extend loans quickly, on more favorable terms, and at less cost and risk to itself. Similarly, a better informed and more cooperative client is likely to get better legal service and at a lower cost.

In addition, the effect of the service may be indirect and not readily traced, so that its value is not adequately understood and cannot be fully measured. Where the renderer of the service increases his expertise there will be, in fact, a change in output. Thus the productivity of the lawyer or engineer cannot be measured in terms of some index such as number of clients serviced, but rather in terms of his effectiveness viewed from the point of view of his client.

In practice, this difficulty in measuring the output of a service organization may result in the value of the output being captured in output of the user. This was recognized by Kuznets (1980) in his recent description of economic growth and development, in which he noted that, historically, gains in productivity from geographically specialized large-scale agriculture and manufacture were due in significant measure to the development of transportation, financial, and communications services that made possible improvements in the modes of production. The principle is applicable, also, in assessing the productivity of the public sector, since better educational services or health services make possible a more knowledgeable and industrious employee and thereby add to the general productivity of the private sector.

A last and related problem arises from our inability to measure properly the service content of goods — not in terms of intermediate but in terms of final output. As will be recognized in Chapter 2, the delivery of goods to consumers is often tied to services (e. g., expert advice in use of the product, financing of the purchase, or warranty and maintenance programs). By not recognizing the joint nature of the offering, traditional national income measures tend to bias the accounts in favor of the goods side. To determine the true extent of this bias would require some major changes in national income accounting procedures.

The Misconception of Spacelessness. For the most part economic analysis is carried out with no regard to the spatial organization of production and consumption, and discussion of growth in services has proceeded within this same spaceless frame of reference. Yet society has become increasingly urbanized, and today over 73 percent of the total population of the economy resides within the boundaries of 266 metropolitan areas (SMSAs). Moreover, these SMSAs differ widely in population and employment, constituting a hierarchy in which a relatively few are very large, a somewhat larger number are of medium size, and an even larger number are relatively small. These places differ not only in size but in economic function and in the level of specialization of many economic activities.

The most general explanation of differences in the role of services among different places is to be found by observing that some services provide for the immediate needs of people and are essentially residentiary in character, while others provide for the special needs of business and government and

are more specialized. In general, residentiary services (e.g.,
grocery stores, beauty parlors, local government) are located
relatively close to households everywhere. Nonresidentiary
services, however, are more concentrated in their location.
They tend to locate in selected metropolitan areas where they
provide for the needs of businesses in surrounding hinter-
lands or for users throughout the nation or the world. These
firms and organizations vary in terms of the degree of their
specialization and the scope of the areas they serve. In general, those services with the broadest markets and the highest
levels of specialization, especially those services catering to the
needs of large corporate headquarters ("producer services"
such as the larger legal firms and financial institutions) have
their highest concentration in the largest places.

As will be shown, a study of some aspects of the changing
nature of the economic specialization of our cities puts considerable strain on the old manufacturing model, in which the
production of goods is at the kernel of the production of
wealth, and the services are a peripheral — almost para-
sitic — element in this picture.

We must begin to re-examine the way the physical landscape has been transformed to fit the demand of a changing
economy, the way the old landscape may have impeded the
blooming of a new one, and the way the present physical
structure may present a barrier to the future. After all, with a
few exceptions the old picture of warehouses and factories
crammed together in the center of the business district is a
part of the recent past in many cities. Yet the rise of office
buildings is revolutionizing their skylines very rapidly.

Lastly, since some large cities seem to have been more
successful incubators of service growth than other smaller
ones, we ought to be able to learn something from their
experience regarding the special set of agglomeration forces
that are necessary to foster such expansion.

The Services in the U. S. Economy:
A Profound Transformation

Against this background of misconceptions and obsolete con-
ceptualizations, we have begun to rethink the economy's shift
toward services as a transformation relating both to *what we*

produce and *how we produce*. This dualism can be further specified in terms of seven propositions.

1. There has been a major shift in *what the economy produces*, involving a shift toward services. This shift as it relates to consumption has involved not so much a major increase in freestanding services as one in services provided jointly with goods, resulting in a stronger identification of the product in the mind of the consumer. This trend toward greater *product differentiation* has come about as a result of both changing consumer demand (rising income and greater consumer desire to break the fetters of an increasingly homogenized life style) and increasing producer emphasis on opening new markets and preserving market shares.

2. Still, a number of freestanding consumer services have demonstrated steady growth (for instance, hotels, restaurants, travel) at the same time that others have experienced sharp declines (household help, barber shops, cleaning and laundry shops). This explains the rather "soft" aggregate growth record found among consumer services provided by the private sector. But the growth demonstrated by those services that have been most amenable to some form of "industrialization" (e.g., restaurants, hotels, travel services) is worthy of note since it indicates, again, changes in consumer demand and a basic transformation in the ability of large firms to capitalize on scale economies by operating on a multi-unit basis (see 4 below).

3. There has been a powerful growth in the provision of health and education services, reflected in a vigorous expansion both of the nonprofit sector and of part of the government sector. Treating this transformation as an increase in final demand of individual consumers, as is traditionally done, is somewhat misleading, however, since expansion of these services is as much a component of the transformation in how we produce as of the transformation in what we produce. Indeed, the rise of health and education is very much a reflection of our society's ever expanding emphasis on investment in human capital (see 7 below).

4. There has been a transformation in the way we organize the productive system of the economy, involving a shift in

functional emphasis from the plant or the service delivery establishment to the central offices of the firm (its headquarters, regional, or divisional offices). This transformation in *how we produce* can itself be regarded as reflecting at once a shift in technology, in labor markets, in consumer markets, and in organizational emphasis.

The introduction of automated and computer-based technologies has ushered in a revolution that is still in its infancy. But the utilization of automated equipment in industries as varied as petrochemicals and electronics[2] and the major retooling of the assembly lines of automobile manufacturers are giving us some sense of where the trend is taking us in goods manufacturing. Large numbers of workers are being pulled out of the manufacturing shop, while production supervision is being moved into the control rooms and the engineering and drafting offices where highly skilled, highly educated professionals and technicians oversee the process.

Interestingly enough, this technological revolution is not limited to manufacturing itself. In a number of consumer services, formerly the nearly exclusive domain of small entrepreneurs, the process of service delivery is increasingly being routinized, standardized, and "industrialized," to use the terms of business theoretician Theodore Levitt (Levitt 1980), while major functions of planning and development, capital allocation, control and management, purchasing, and franchising are being centralized in overhead offices with the help of computer technologies. In addition, the central offices that plan and coordinate the operation of the manufacturing plants or service delivery establishments are themselves being transformed through a rationalization of routine tasks with the help of "office of the future" kinds of technologies.

Meanwhile, the sharpening of intercorporate competition and the desire to reach ever broader markets have made it imperative for the large corporation to invest greater amounts of resources in its planning of the different phases of the product cycle and in its efforts to reach the consumer through advertising and consumer financing. This further reinforces the shift of attention away from the establishment to the central offices of the firm, where economies of scale in the provision of concomitant services can best be realized.

Finally, the very rise of the large corporation calls for the firm to pay much greater attention to itself — its own administration, internal control and management, relations with employees, and short- and long-term planning — in a corporate world where tens of thousands of employees may be employed in scores of establishments, in a multitude of locations and, at times, in a number of countries.

As suggested, these and other factors have brought a vigorous growth of specialized "producer services" both in-house (in the central administrative facilities of the corporation) and out-of-house (among producer service firms). From the point of view of a reconceptualization, it is important to note that this major dimension of change is primarily a transformation at the level of intermediate outputs.

5.   This rise of producer services activity has been reinforced by the increasing importance of the role played by the government sector in economic life. Directly, the public sector has taken on a major responsibility in areas as varied as research and development or the financing of foreign trade (through the ExIm bank, assistance programs to foreign countries, and a host of related devices). More indirectly, government, as a key mediator of the many conflicts of interests arising from changes within the economy, has impelled the growth of a multitude of producer-service-like functions designed to regulate competition, protect consumer interests, defend employees' working conditions, further the goals of equal opportunity, and even protect its own interest against the pressure of both producers and consumers. Here again, the trend has been toward a multiplication of producer-service-like functions designed to deal with the increasing complexity of our society.

6.   The transformations in what and how we produce are resulting in changes regarding where we organize production and consumption, in geographical terms. Different kinds of work activities are very location-specific, with the result that a powerful transformation is underway in how we organize economic activities of the urban system. Services are playing a leading role in this process, as different types of service activities locate in different types and sizes of place (see Chapter 5). We also note that the metropolitan residential landscape is

undergoing some major changes (e.g. gentrification) that are altering the old, simple, suburb– middle classes and central-city – lower classes dichotomy. These observations raise broad but important questions about the changing social and economic functions of our cities, and more specific ones as to their role as incubators of new economic activity.

7.   Likewise, the transformations in what and how we produce are resulting in changes in the way we organize the work process and distribute income. First, there has been a continuous and enlarged investment of resources in people since the 1930s. This says something very important about the ongoing shift in our society: from an earlier focus on investment in physical capital to a rising concern for careful optimization of investment in human skills. Second, the work structures that have emerged in the various services do not resemble the old, factory-based, blue-collarlike occupational structures of a previous era. Here, our old conceptual map of work and work organizations appears largely irrelevant for predicting the future. Finally, it seems that these profound changes in occupational structure, the major increase in women's participation in the labor force and the growing importance of part-time work are transforming the structure of income distribution no less dramatically than the ways in which individuals choose to organize their lives (greater flexibility in leisure time or new developmental career patterns).

Some Empirical Evidence of the Transformation
As an initial approach to examining some of the trends highlighted above, it is useful to classify economic activities by general type of output. To analyze changes in the employment structure of the economy we use a classification scheme of industries similar to that advanced by Singelmann (1978). Table 1.1 indicates how the various two-digit SIC groups have been reorganized to distinguish between services that are primarily intermediate as opposed to primarily final outputs, and also to acknowledge the different institutional settings – private, public, and nonprofit – under which services are provided. This procedure permits identification of six groups of services: the *distributive* services, the *retail* services, the *non-*

profit services, the *producer* services, the *mainly consumer* services, and the *government* services.

This scheme is used consistently throughout this study, with three small adaptations depending on statistical sources. Where the source permits it, the employees of the central administrative offices and auxiliary establishments (CAO & A) of firms in the major industrial sectors (mining, construction, manufacturing, TCU, fire, and services) are isolated and examined in conjunction with the producer services (Chapters 3 and 5). In the chapter on labor (Chapter 4), education and

---

Table 1.1   Classification of Industries for Gross National Product and Employment Analysis

Agriculture, extractive and transformative industries

Agriculture	SIC 01, 02, 07, 08, 09
Extractive and Transformative	
Mining	SIC 10, 11, 12, 13, 14
Construction	SIC 15, 16, 17
Manufacturing	SIC 20 to 39

Services

Distributive Services	
TCU	SIC 40 to 49
Wholesale	SIC 50, 51
Retail Services	SIC 52 to 59
Nonprofit services	
Health	SIC 80
Education	SIC 82
Producer services	
Finance	SIC 60 to 67
Insurance	
Real estate	
Business services	SIC 73
Legal services	SIC 81
Membership organizations	SIC 86
Miscellaneous professional services	SIC 89
Social services	SIC 83 after 1974
Mainly consumer services	
Hotels and other lodging places	SIC 70
Personal services	SIC 72
Auto repair, services, and garages	SIC 75
Miscellaneous repair services	SIC 76
Motion pictures	SIC 78
Amusements and recreation services	SIC 79, 84
Private households	SIC 88
Government and government enterprises	SIC 91 to 97

Source: Adapted from J. Singlemann, *From Agriculture to Services* (Beverly Hills, California: Sage Publications, 1978), p. 31.

Table 1.2 Distribution of Full-Time Equivalent Employees among Industries, 1929 to 1977

Industry classifications	1929 Employee Number	1929 Employee Share (%)	1939 Employee Number	1939 Employee Share (%)
Agriculture, extractive and transformative	15,857	44.87	14,386	40.06
Agriculture	2,952	8.35	2,368	6.59
Extractive and transformative	12,905	36.52	12,018	33.46
Mining	993	2.81	832	2.32
Construction	1,484	4.20	1,219	3.39
Manufacturing	10,428	29.51	9,967	27.75
Services	19,481	55.13	21,528	59.94
Distributive services	5,535	15.66	4,634	12.90
Transportation	2,873	8.13	1,990	5.54
Communication	538	1.52	423	1.18
Utilities	493	1.39	445	1.24
Wholesale	1,631	4.62	1,776	4.94
Retail services	4,215[a]	11.93[a]	4,389[a]	12.22[a]
Nonprofit services	653	1.85	787	2.19
Health	429	1.21	522	1.45
Education	224	0.63	265	0.74
Producer services	2,068	5.85	2,094	5.83
FIRE	1,415	4.00	1,376	3.83
Other producer services	653	1.85	718	2.00
Mainly consumer services	3,806	10.77	3,452	9.61
Hotels and personal services	1,004	2.84	954	2.66
Auto and miscellaneous repair services	59[b]	0.17[b]	58[b]	0.16[b]
Motion pictures, amusement, and recreation	395	1.12	345	0.96
Private households	2,348	6.64	2,075	5.78
Government	3,204	9.07	6,172	17.19
Public education	1,082	3.06	1,224	3.41
Domestic Industries	35,338	100.00	35,914	100.00

[a] Includes auto services.
[b] Excludes auto services.
Source: U.S. Department of Commerce, Bureau of Economic Analysis, *The National Income and Product Account of the United States, 1929–74 Statistical Tables*; and *Survey of Current Business*, July 1978.

health employees of the government sector are regrouped with those of the nonprofit sector, while employment in restaurants is taken out of the retail sector and brought under the mainly consumer service heading.

Despite its improvement over the Fisher-Clark three-sector model,* this classification scheme does not distinguish per-

---

*Primary (agriculture and mining), secondary (construction and manufacturing), and tertiary (services) sectors.

Table 1.2 (continued)

1948 Employee		1959 Employee		1969 Employee		1977 Employee	
Number	Share (%)	Number	Share (%)	Number	Share (%)	Number	Share (%)
20,864	43.49	21,271	38.34	25,055	35.09	25,132	31.60
2,072	4.31	1,764	3.18	1,240	1.74	1,510	1.90
18,792	39.08	19,507	35.16	23,815	33.35	23,622	29.70
993	2.06	709	1.28	610	0.85	810	1.02
2,278	4.74	2,761	4.98	3,452	4.83	3,641	4.58
15,521	32.27	16,037	28.91	19,753	27.66	19,171	24.10
27,226	56.61	34,205	61.66	46,350	64.91	54,403	68.40
6,512	13.54	6,742	12.15	7,832	10.97	9,034	11.36
2,854	5.93	2,494	4.50	2,634	3.69	2,654	3.34
739	1.54	799	1.44	1,001	1.40	1,125	1.41
528	1.10	594	1.07	651	0.91	734	0.92
2,391	4.97	2,855	5.15	3,546	4.97	4,521	5.68
6,047	12.57	7,045	12.70	9,283	13.00	11,276	14.18
1,254	2.61	1,954	3.52	3,338	4.67	5,043	6.34
825	1.72	1,366	2.46	2,375	3.33	4,128	5.19
429	0.89	588	1.06	963	1.35	915	1.15
2,912	6.06	4,566	8.23	7,162	10.03	9,515	11.96
1,678	3.49	2,471	4.45	3,415	4.78	4,209	5.29
1,234	2.57	2,095	3.78	3,747	5.25	5,306	6.67
3,689	7.67	3,592	6.47	4,108	5.75	3,966	4.99
1,305	2.71	1,246	2.25	1,617	2.26	1,591	2.00
349	0.73	360	0.65	520	0.73	685	0.86
461	0.96	394	0.71	504	0.71	676	0.85
1,574	3.27	1,592	2.87	1,467	2.05	1,014	1.27
6,812	14.16	10,306	18.58	14,627	20.48	15,569	19.57
1,418	2.95	2,347	4.23	4,050	5.67	5,121	6.44
48,090	100.00	55,476	100.00	71,405	100.00	79,535	100.00

fectly among functions. Many of the services cater both to producers and final consumers. Thus, much of the output of the hotel or restaurant industry serves a consumer as well as a producer demand, just as accountants or lawyers deliver services to both private individuals and firms. In the case of finance and insurance, whose dealings with consumers and producers are highly interdependent, the problem is even thornier (Goldstein 1980).

The most important observation is that the major shifts that have occurred within the American economy result from the reduction in employment within agriculture, the decline of jobs in manufacturing plants, and the rise in the role of non-profit, government, and producer services. What is most dramatic when contrasted with generally accepted notions is that consumer services, popularly regarded as the most important activities involved in the growth of services in the affluent late 20th century society, have not grown rapidly, whereas producer services have played a major role.

Some highlights of the main statistical findings regarding the shifts in employment from 1929 until today are helpful here (see Table 1.2).

Between 1929 and 1977 the share of the U.S. employment accounted for by nonprofit services grew steadily from 1.8 to 6.3 percent. This does not include educational and health services provided by the government sector, which in 1977 accounted for more than 6 percent.

While the share of employment in the producer services remained relatively constant until the late 1940s, it began to grow steadily starting in the early 1950s. The share went from 5.8 percent in 1929 to 6 percent in 1948, and up to 12 percent in 1977.

The share of employment in the public sector grew fairly rapidly after the 1930s and began to stabilize only in recent years. Overall, it has risen from a 9 percent share of the employed labor force in 1929 to almost 20 percent in 1977.

The share of employment in the mainly consumer services declined over the 1929–1977 period (from more than 10 percent to 5 percent). This resulted from the rapid decline of private household workers while other consumer services retained and in some cases enlarged their shares.

The share of employment in the retail sector remained relatively steady over time (12 percent in 1929, 13 percent in 1969), and began to grow again during the 1970s (14.2 percent in 1977).

The share of employment in the distributive services declined over the entire period (15.6 percent in 1929, 11.4 percent in 1977).

Table 1.3 Annual Rate of Growth of Full-Time Equivalent Employees by Industry, 1929 to 1977

Industry classifications	1929– 1939	1939– 1947	1948– 1959	1959– 1969	1969– 1977
Domestic industries	0.1	3.4	1.3	2.5	1.3
Agriculture, extractive and transformative	-0.8	4.3	0.1	1.6	0.1
Agriculture	-1.8	-1.8	-1.2	-2.5	2.5
Extractive and transformative	-0.6	5.3	0.3	2.0	-0.1
Manufacturing	-0.4	5.4	0.3	2.1	-0.3
Services	1.0	2.8	2.0	3.0	2.0
Distributive services	-1.5	4.2	0.3	1.5	1.8
TCU	-2.4	4.4	-0.5	0.9	0.6
Wholesale	0.8	3.8	1.6	2.1	3.0
Retail services	0.4	4.5	1.4	2.8	2.4
Nonprofit services	1.8	4.3	4.1	5.5	5.2
Health	1.9	4.9	4.6	5.6	7.1
Education	1.6	3.0	2.9	5.0	-0.6
Producer services	0.1	3.7	4.1	4.5	3.6
Mainly consumer services	-0.8	0.2	-0.2	1.3	-0.4
Private household	-1.1	-2.4	0.1	-0.7	-3.3
Government	6.3	1.1	3.8	3.5	0.7
Public education	1.2	1.3	4.6	5.6	2.9

Source: See Table 1.2.

The share of employment in manufacturing, after peaking in the late 1940s, declined dramatically in the decades which followed (29.5 percent in 1929, 32.3 percent in 1948, and 24 percent in 1977).

Table 1.3, which presents rates of employment growth during the past five decades, further underlines widely varying experiences among different industrial groupings. It indicates quite clearly that the treatment of the growth of services as a monolithic shift within the economy is an unwarranted simplification. If we are to understand what is taking place, a more carefully specified conceptualization is required.

The second set of statistics (Table 1.4) presents data on the changes in the distribution of Gross National Product originating in each sector between 1948 and 1977. The most remarkable observation relates to the comparison of the share of national product generated by the manufacturing, mining, and construction sectors combined (i.e., the extractive and

Table 1.4 Percentage Distribution of Gross National Product by Industries, 1947–1977 (in billions of 1972 dollars)

Industry classifications	1947 $	1947 %	1969 $	1969 %	1977 $	1977 %
Agriculture, extractive and transformative	175.1	37.38	388.3	35.99	437.4	32.81
Agriculture	26.1	5.57	33.0	3.06	38.3	2.87
Extractive and transformative	149.0	31.81	355.3	32.93	399.1	29.94
Manufacturing[a]	114.9	24.53	276.2	25.60	322.3	24.18
Services	293.6	62.68	690.9	64.03	881.1	66.09
Distributive services	62.6	13.36	161.8	15.00	220.1	16.51
Retail services	51.8	11.06	105.5	9.78	131.8	9.89
Nonprofit services	12.5	2.67	38.6	3.58	53.8	4.04
Producer services[b]	72.6	15.50	197.0	18.26	268.2	20.12
Mainly consumer services	25.6	5.47	36.2	3.35	41.5	3.11
Government and government enterprises	68.5	14.62	151.8	14.07	165.7	12.43
Residual and rest of the world	–0.3	–0.06	–0.2	–0.20	14.6	1.10
All Industries	468.4	100.00	1,079.0	100.00	1,333.1	100.00

[a]Includes CAO & A (central administrative offices and auxiliary establishments).
[b]Excludes CAO & A.

Source: U.S. Department of Commerce, Bureau of Economic Analysis, *The National Income and Product Accounts of the United States, 1929–74 Statistical Tables* (Washington, D.C.: USGPO, 1977), Table 6.2; "Gross National Product by Major Industry. Workfile 1205-02-03." Unpublished material provided by BEA.; and U.S. National Income and Product Accounts: Revised Estimates, 1975–77," *Survey of Current Business*, July 1978, Table 6.2, p. 52.

transformative industries) with that of the producer services. Freestanding producer services are shown to account for 20 percent of the national product. If we adjust this share upward to include the producer-service-like national product originating within the Central Administrative Offices of firms (which we estimate to be at least 5 percent of the GNP), we conclude that in 1977, 25 percent of the national product originated in the combined producer services and producer-service-like functions, as compared to an almost equal share of GNP originating in the extractive and transformative activities *stricto sensu*. By comparison, a similar breakdown for 1947 (the earliest available year in our data) showed a split of 15 percent versus 30 percent between the former and the latter.

The second observation derived from this table in conjunction with Table 1.2 is the marked discrepancy between GNP shares and employment shares. The share of GNP originating in the government sector, the mainly consumer services, and the nonprofit sector have tended to be *lower* than their respective employment shares; the share of GNP originating in the producer services has tended to be *much higher* than the corresponding share of employment. This observation does not lend itself to easy interpretation, however, since it reflects some combination of differences in levels of wage rates, capital intensiveness, and productivity in the various industries.

The final set of statistics presented here is borrowed from research by John Myers (1980). Table 1.5 summarizes the share of GNP accounted for by goods and services by *industry of origin* and by *final product* in three selected years — 1929, 1948, and 1978. In the latter year, services measured in terms of industry of origin accounted for 66 percent of GNP; when measured as a share of final product, only 46 percent.

These empirical findings support some of the propositions postulated earlier regarding the rise of the services in our advanced capitalistic economy. At the same time, they suggest some of the limitations inherent in any detailed analysis based on the data generated by the national income and product accounting system (for instance, the difficulty of breaking out the service content of goods, as discussed earlier in proposition 1).

Table 1.5   **Relative Importance of Services in GNP in Current Dollars, as Indicated by Industry of Origin and Type of Final Product, 1929, 1948, and 1978**

	1929	1948	1978
	(percentage of GNP in each year)		
Industry of origin			
Goods producing	41.0	45.8	34.2
Service producing	59.0	54.2	65.8
Type of final product			
Goods	54.3	59.6	43.7
Services	34.7	29.6	45.6
Structures	11.0	10.8	10.7

Source: U.S. Department of Commerce, Bureau of Economic Analysis, *The National Income and Product Accounts of the U.S. 1929–1974.* From John Myers, "GNP: Perspectives on Services," 1980.

The Transformation in Historical Perspective

Viewed from a broad historical perspective, the remarkable aspect of the transformation is the timing of the different shifts. Table 1.6 presents data on sectoral shares of employment for the earlier 1870– 1930 period. Once Tables 1.6 and 1.2 (1929– 1977) are examined together, they offer a truly revealing picture of more than a century of economic change.[3]

The two tables show three basic trends for the 1870– 1977 period, well known to any economic historian: the continuous reduction of the share of employment in agriculture; the sustained growth in manufacturing, followed in the last two decades by the beginning of a decline in this major sector; and the steady expansion of the role of the services sector. More important, however, is what they also indicate about the se-

Table 1.6 Percentage Distribution of Gainfully Employed Workers, 1870–1930

Industry classifications	1870 Share	1880 Share	1890 Share	1900 Share	1910 Share	1920 Share	1930 Share
Agriculture, extractive and transformative	75.3	75.6	71.5	68.7	64.2	62.4	54.5
Agriculture	50.4	50.6	43.2	38.1	32.1	27.7	22.6
Extractive and transformative	24.9	25.0	28.3	30.6	32.1	34.7	31.9
Mining	1.6	1.8	2.0	2.7	2.9	3.0	2.4
Construction	5.8	4.8	6.1	5.8	6.4	5.3	6.4
Manufacturing	17.5	18.4	20.2	22.1	22.8	26.4	23.1
Services	24.7	24.3	28.5	31.3	35.8	37.6	45.4
Distributive and retail services	N.A.	N.A.	N.A.	N.A.	18.1	20.1	22.9
TCU	5.0	5.0	6.5	7.3	8.8	10.2	10.2
Wholesale and retail trade	6.4[a]	7.1[a]	8.5[a]	9.6[a]	9.3	9.9	12.7
Nonprofit services	1.5	1.9	2.2	2.3	2.5	2.8	3.5
Education[b]	1.5	1.9	2.2	2.3	2.5	2.8	3.5
Producer services	N.A.	N.A.	N.A.	N.A.	3.5	4.5	6.7
FIRE	N.A.[c]	N.A.[c]	N.A.[c]	N.A.[c]	1.4	1.9	3.0
Other producer services	1.1	1.1	1.5	1.7	2.1	2.6	3.7
Mainly consumer services	9.3	8.4	9.2	9.5	10.2	8.1	10.1
Personal services	2.0	2.1	2.7	3.4	4.2	4.0	5.2
Domestic services	7.3	6.3	6.5	6.1	6.0	4.1	4.9
Government	0.8	0.8	0.8	1.0	1.5	2.2	2.2
Domestic industries	100.0	100.0	100.0	100.0	100.0	100.0	100.0

N.A.: not available
[a] Includes FIRE.
[b] Includes education provided by the public sector.
[c] FIRE is included in Wholesale and retail trade.
Source: U.S. Department of Commerce, Bureau of the Census, *Historical Statistics of the U.S., Colonial Times to 1970* (Washington D.C.: USGPO, 1976).

quence of growth leadership among the services: first, in the distributive and retail services; second, in the government sector; and third and most recent, in the nonprofit and the producer services.

Kuznets (1980) has argued quite convincingly that the transition from an agrarian to an industrial society implied a dramatic transformation in the way we organized production and consumption spatially. Industrialization meant a massive geographical restructuring of our productive capacity and the beginning of a locational divorce between points of production and points of consumption. Residents of cities became dependent on foodstuffs produced in the countryside at the same time that farmers needed the goods and equipment produced by largely urban manufacturers. Along with growth of manufacturing and spatial reorganization, the early industrial society had created a need for a network of distributive and retail services. Thus it comes as no surprise to note that rapid growth of the distributive and retail services accompanied the development of manufacturing in the early period of industrialism.

Nobody will deny that the role of government as we know it today is largely the outcome of a transformation that came about as a result of the economic crises of the 1930s, although the 1910s and 1920s may have given some early indications as to what was to follow (viz., the rise of regulatory activity or the rise of public education during the so-called "reform era"). Moreover, it is important to recognize that much of the transformation initiated in the thirties paved the way for the most recent changes associated with the rise of the nonprofit sector and of the producer services.

Having been called in to resolve the deadlocks of the 1930s, the public sector proceeded to become increasingly involved in fundamental economic processes:

1. by appropriating a much larger share of the national product to redirect demand in areas as diverse as housing, road construction, public works and, later on, industrial R & D, military and aerospace equipment;

2. by answering the need for greater workmen's protection, first by establishing a system of unemployment compensation and then by erecting the foundations of what would

become a broadly based system of social insurance and welfare;

3. by answering the need for greater social equality
through use of its financial and legal power to foster more
equitable economic development (e.g., rural electrification
and secondary highways), fairer income redistribution and
later on greater social equality of opportunities (through programs aimed at both access to higher education and equiliza-
tion of employment opportunities);

4. by imposing a more stringent regulatory framework on
business to curb what was then seen as excesses impeding
society's desire to achieve smoother and fairer economic
growth.

Aside from the rechanneling of a major portion of the
national product, the other major impact of this transformation in the role of the public sector was a dramatic rise in its
share of employment.

While both Kuznets (1980) and Abramovitz (1972) have
argued that the expansion of the nonprofit sector since the
1930s is an extension of the rising public demand for greater
social equality, they have also been careful to note that the
pace of technological innovation in our society has awakened
an equally powerful demand on the part of producers for a
healthier and better educated workforce more fit to deal with
the requirements of modern technology.

The recent growth of the producer services must also be
understood in terms of certain changes that the large corporations were forced to make as a result of the 1930s experience.
Until then, the very large corporation, concentrating on relatively restricted product lines (steel, rubber, automobiles, oil,
chemicals, etc.) had departed little from the textbook example
of the monopolistic or oligopolistic firm. Two very powerful
forces acted to change this model of corporate development.
First, as many firms learned the hard way during the reces-
sion, the single-product orientation was accompanied by a
high degree of sensitivity to cyclical fluctuations. Second, and
as noted earlier, consumers saw the development toward
monopoly as a serious threat to their interests and sent a very
powerful message to government to alter this course of events.

What followed in the next decades was a major shift toward

corporate diversification which, some argued at the time, would provide an answer to both of these demands (1) by reintroducing some elements of competition in areas where it was tending to become lost and (2) by providing for the formation of corporate entities less sensitive to the surgings of the business cycle. Whether these benefits ever fully developed is another matter, but we would argue that this early drive toward corporate diversification, along with the more recent forces of change treated at greater length in the various chapters of this monograph (transformation of the market, additional government regulation, technology, internationalization, etc.), explain much of the growth of the producer services and of producer-service-like functions in the postwar era.

Plan of the Study

In presenting the plan of this study on the rise of the services in the U.S. economy, it is important to make clear that we have not tried to tackle directly such major economic issues as declining growth rates, productivity, unemployment, or inflation. We did not believe we could make any significant contribution to measurement problems within the short time frame under which this study was conducted, although we hope that what we have learned may shed some light on these matters. Indeed, some of these issues are brought back into the discussion of Chapter 6, in which a set of preliminary propositions concerning a reconceptualization of theory and policy issues is put forth.

What we have begun to study is the nature of a complex set of transformations at work within the system. We must observe at the outset that although there appears to be a diminution in growth, there seems to have occurred no slackening in the pace at which change has been taking place within our society. Accordingly, we have assumed that something useful can be learned by examining the nature of ongoing changes, changes which appear, at least to a considerable extent, in the form of a rising importance of services. The hope is that we have begun to recognize discontinuities, detect new trends, and develop useful generalizations that will contribute to better theory and more effective public policy.

Following this introduction, this monograph is organized in five chapters:

2. The Changing Nature of Consumption
3. Changing Markets, Changing Firms, and the Rise of Producer Services
4. Employment: Occupational and Earnings Structure and the Changing Nature of Work
5. The Changing Urban Landscape and the Location of Economic Activities
6. Reconceptualization: Building Blocks for New Bridges Between Theory and Policy

Chapter 2 addresses the changing patterns of consumption and the growing importance of service-goods complementarity. The increasing importance of product differentiation is examined and contributing forces are identified. The evidence suggests that we are leaving an era in which systemwide, homogeneous mass consumption has been emphasized and are entering one of increasingly segmented and personalized modes of consumption.

Chapter 3, "Changing Markets, Changing Firms, and the Rise of Producer Services," centers on two concepts, rising market size and rising firm size, the forces which have lead to the vigorous expansion and multiplication of producer services both in- and out-of-house. Also discussed is the shift that has occurred in large and medium-sized corporations from a focus on economizing in plant and service-delivery establishments to a concern for achieving scale economies at the higher firm levels relating to administration, product development, and planning.

Chapter 4, "Employment," points to the changing nature of work associated with the rise of the services and the related transformation of both the occupational and the earnings structures. It suggests that new work arrangements and new occupational structures are emerging, of which we have barely begun to outline the contours.

Likewise, Chapter 5, "The Changing Urban Landscape," takes note of the profound transformation undergone by our urban system. Urbanization, it is argued, can be seen both mirroring and contributing to the ongoing transformation. On the one hand, the changes undergone by the city merely reflect — albeit in a much sharper way — the many shifts observed in the economy at large. On the other, the city is itself a "tool" to organize consumption and production in our society. The ability to transform our economy and the extent to which new modes of consumption and production will arise are thus in part dependent on our capacity to transform our mode of urban life.

Chapter 6, "Reconceptualization," takes note of the failure of traditional economic theory to suggest new directions for policy. Capitalizing on some of the findings of the previous chapters, it begins to articulate conceptual blocks around which a new and better-fitted theory of our advanced economy might be organized.

Although we recognize their importance, three issues which have their place in this kind of analytical work are not addressed directly in this volume: technology, the public sector, and the internationalization of our economy. Technology and the public sector are touched on to the extent that they have a bearing on some of the issues dealt with. Technology, for instance, is said to have been a fundamental force in the reorganization of work and of the occupational structure (Chapter 4) and in furthering the shift of emphasis from the establishment to the central office of the firm (Chapter 3). The public sector is dealt with to the extent that it is an integral part of the rise of producer services (Chapter 3) or of the rising importance of human capital in our economy (Chapter 4). Obviously, this does not cover the full extent of the transformation brought about by the rise of the public sector; for instance, the increasing importance of nonmarket transactions in an essentially market-based economic system. The issue of internationalization of the economy is addressed only peripherally, although we recognize that the rise of the services in the U.S. economy is in part a response to the need to facilitate the financing and marketing of an even larger international flow of goods and to provide the special expertise and technical infrastructure that allows major corporations to penetrate foreign markets.

Notes

[1] See Table 1.1 for a more-detailed presentation of the industry classification used in this monograph.

[2] See the example of Texas Instruments' automated factories in Lubbock, Midland-Odessa, and Abilene (*Business Week,* September 18, 1978).

[3] Differences in sources explain most of the discrepancies between the two tables. Table 1.6 for the 1870–1930 period is based on a count of "gainful workers." Table 1.2 for the 1929–1977 period is based on a count of "full-time equivalent. employees." See Singelmann (1978) for discussion of these differences.

2. The Changing Nature of Consumption

While it is widely recognized that growth in population and per capita income under conditions of mass production and mass distribution have brought about increasingly higher levels of consumption, it is not immediately clear just what role has been played by services in consumption. The popular notion that we now live in a service economy, in the sense that consumer services purchased directly in the marketplace constitute a major share of our budgets, is simply not borne out by the facts.

Services are playing an increasingly critical role in consumption, however. It is a role both direct and indirect: indirect, in the sense that the design, production, promotion, and distribution of goods and services under conditions of product differentiation and ever stronger consumer orientation require a heavy input of producer services both out-of-house and in-house; direct, in that services are coupled with goods by producers as a joint offering in the marketplace and that the consumption of services plays a vital complementary role to the consumption of goods. To understand the role of services requires an examination of the nature of the modern consumer economy and of the principal forces that drive it.

Factors of Change: The Push Toward Variety
It is a major paradox that the American economy is widely regarded as becoming increasingly standardized at the very

time that the choices of goods and services available to the consumer are increasing almost exponentially.[1]

Government statistics do not capture this characteristic of increasing variety, but the evidence lies on every hand. Philip Morris established its reputation as producer of a single brand of cigarettes during the years prior to 1954. By 1970, the combinations of brands and options relating to size, filter, menthol, and level of tar produced by the company constituted a selection of 16 variations (Toffler 1970). General Motors and Ford in each of their divisions offer a variety of options of bodies, engines, transmissions, colors, and a host of special features that, in large measure, permit the customer to tailor the car to his individual taste. General Mills has moved far from its original concentration on processing grains to a product line that today includes hundreds of prepared foodstuffs.

The list can be extended almost indefinitely, far beyond conventional household goods and services. A score of years or more ago the writer purchased one of Eastern Airline's original "Happy Holidays" package tours, which included three components: transportation, hotel accommodations, and a rum drink at the airport of a Caribbean island. Today airlines, travel agents, hotel chains, and even universities offer a variety of vacation and travel packages, ranging from economy to luxury in price and specifications and including destinations as accessible as Atlantic City and as remote as the Arctic Circle. In the field of publications there has been a dramatic trend toward reaching out to individual markets. *Vogue* now publishes nine separate regional editions and *The Wall Street Journal,* four. Special interest magazines for the hobbyist, for the sports fan, and for a host of different cultural and vocational groups have proliferated at the same time that general audience magazines, such as *Life* and *Look,* have been discontinued or forced to sharply revise their format. Radio entertainment now tends to be offered to the public in a differentiated format; some stations broadcast classical music, others specialize in rock, country western, or news, or cater to blacks or to ethnic groups who prefer to hear their own language and folk music. In the field of education we have moved far from the old, relatively standardized curriculum of a quarter-century ago to a highly varied offering.[2]

Alvin Toffler has stressed advances in technology as a major factor contributing to increased product variety, and quoted Boris Yavitz, former industrial engineer and currently dean of the Columbia University Graduate School of Business, as stating almost a decade ago, "Numerically controlled machines can readily shift from one product model to another by a simple change of programs . . . short product runs become economically feasible."[3] Martin Starr (1979) has pointed out the remarkable economies that are now available for production through modules within the plant, which permits scale economies along with product differentiation in the fabrication of complex products.

Clearly, the new computer-based technology has enormously facilitated the shift toward product differentiation, but an even more significant development is the changing nature of the market itself. The forces that have broadened the market included not only a doubling real per capita income and a 20 percent increase in total population between 1960 to 1977, but also rapid urbanization that has served to increase the density of markets.

The movement from regional and subregional markets toward a single national system stems from a number of factors of which only a few can be mentioned here. Three wars in which young men and women were transported back and forth across the continent, the management policies of large corporations which have dictated frequent transfers of executive personnel often over considerable distances, the rapid rise of jet travel, the construction of the interstate highway system and the increase in automobile ownership, and, most especially, the universal acceptance of television as a principal source of entertainment and information, all have contributed to the development of tastes which are largely national in scope.

In a sense this reduction of regional differences has worked toward homogenization. Clearly, it has facilitated both mass production and mass distribution. People wear the same clothes, drive the same cars, eat the same food, visit the same motels and restaurants, and tell the same jokes in California as in the Carolinas. Yet, at the same time, it has created the necessary market conditions for an even freer play of forces making for product differentiation and a proliferation of new products and services.

It is here that the demand theory of Kelvin Lancaster (1979) sheds considerable light on the process at work. Lancaster observes that products are purchased for the multiple characteristics they possess, that products may typically be varied to provide somewhat different bundles of characteristics, and that consumers differ in their individual preferences for these characteristics.

Given these conditions, the firm can increase sales volume by moving away from a single product, which meets well the needs of only a few, to several variations of the product, each designed to appeal to a different spectrum of the market. It can do so, however, only at some sacrifice in terms of economies of scale. Thus the extent of product differentiation is limited by the size of the market with larger markets creating conditions that both justify and require product differentiation. Larger markets provide demand sufficient to support a larger number of differentiated models. At the same time competition makes it imperative that the seller engage aggressively in a battle within the market place by identifying his product in the buyer's eyes and promoting it (Levitt 1980).

But the market need not be visualized simply as a collection of single individuals, each with a different preference schedule for every existing or potential product. More properly it should be visualized as a collection of subsets of potential customers with similar, though not identical, preference functions and incomes.

The study of subgroupings within society is, of course, the province of the sociologist. Herbert Gans (1975) has identified a number of culture groups and analyzed the manner and the extent to which changes in tastes are transmitted from one group to another. He specifies seven culture groups: high, upper-middle, lower-middle, quasi-folk, "youth," black, and ethnic and demonstrates strong similarities in levels of education and in tastes for music, food, art, entertainment, and literature among individuals who make up each group.

Gans notes that individual tastes differ and that there is a considerable amount of cross-culture consumption. He observes also that there are important tendencies toward fragmentation within culture groups, especially within the lower-middle culture.

The significance of the existence of culture groupings is that they are an important factor contributing to the development of submarkets within which firms must exercise product policy. To the extent that segments represent rich market potentials, firms will tailor their products and promotion policies to reach out to them. To the extent that incomes and/or numbers are small, producers accord them less attention.

The effect of the broadening of the market has been to increase the economic significance of previously dormant or relatively unimportant subcultures. As elements of these subcultures are brought together from coast to coast, market potentials increase and products that cater to their special needs and interest are offered in the market place. The process is abetted by the appearance of periodicals and other literature which serve to bring about increased communication and self-identification.

Factors of Change: Fulfilling Life Style and Personal Identity Needs

The changes taking place in the consumer goods and services markets are extremely complex. Increasing size of market as a force working to bring about product differentiation and the introduction of a broad array of new products and services is but one factor acting to change patterns of consumption. In this section we try to show how rising levels of income have transformed consumer demand.

Some Basic Elements of a Theory of Consumption Behavior. We do not essay to develop a full-blown theory of consumption, but it is important to examine the way in which consumption may be affected by increasing incomes and to note a few of the most important factors that have shaped the evolution of consumption in the postwar period. Even the most elementary demand theory based on assumptions of diminishing utility of increments of consumption of a specific good or service leads to the observation that, with rising income, an individual's total pattern of consumption will include an increasing number of products and services. When we add to this the observation that there are certain wants that take precedence over others because of basic human needs of survival and comfort, and that these wants account for a progressively smaller share of total expenditures as levels of income increase (viz. Engel's early findings regarding expenditures for food), we must then observe that freedom of choice increases with income, resulting in the likelihood that one person's pattern of consumption will differ increasingly from another's as income rises. If Jones and Brown each have incomes of $10,000, their patterns are likely to be similar, because basic needs do not differ greatly; but if each enjoys an increase in income to $50,000, consumption patterns will tend to diverge sharply. Thus, rising income creates increasing amounts of discretionary income within the economy — income that may be used to experiment with new patterns of consumption.

Abraham Maslow (1968) has set forth a model of human behavior in which man's first priority, to fulfill needs for biological survival, is followed by a succession of higher needs. As each lower-order need is fulfilled, "desire" shifts to the next higher level. His hierarchical sequence is as follows: (1) biological survival, (2) security, (3) social affiliation, (4) self-esteem, and (5) self-actualization.

As Karasek (1980a) notes, the most important difference between this view and that of conventional economics is a point not emphasized by Maslow: there are fundamental differences in the processes by which these needs are fulfilled. Many of Maslow's needs are satisfied through economic goods (e.g., the need for food and shelter) that require scarce resources — what one person consumes may not be consumed by another. On the other hand, some of Maslow's higher-order needs do not face the same constraints of scarcity: social affiliations seem to grow abundantly wherever there is human contact (except, of course, when conflicts over scarce resources arise), and one person's "social affiliation" certainly does not reduce his friend's feeling of "affiliation"; indeed, it may augment it (Karasek 1980b). Here consumption is not "rival."

Our discussion of a consumption hierarchy is analogous in format to Maslow but adds several simplifying principles to link our levels together analytically. We propose three levels of consumption needs (Karasek 1980b): basic needs (for biological survival), convenience needs, and "life style/identity" needs. This last category of needs reflects man's "ultimate goal": to develop his human potential by growth of his competences and interests in dealing with the surrounding world (similar to Maslow's highest-order need, self-actualization). Man's only constraint in pursuit of this ultimate goal is the limitation of his own physical time and energy. But before man is interested in devoting his energies toward "life style/identity" needs, he must fulfill basic and convenience needs (similar to Maslow's ideas). Basic need satisfaction is necessary to develop a "plateau" of minimal well-being for higher-order functions. No higher-order consumption than eating is conceivable or desirable to the starving.

Because life style/identity satisfaction is ultimately limited by available time, "time" must be salvaged from drudgery and discomfort and turned into "good time," which is the scarce usable input to a person's "production" of life style/identity satisfaction. Thus, the second level of consumption goods serves this purpose: convenience goods reduce the drudgery, sickness, or other incumbrances on use of free time. Some convenience goods expand free time (i.e., increase discretionary time). Home appliances and other convenience goods (or comforts) reduce stress and care. Semiprepared foods reduce the labor burden of perfunctory meal preparation. A car (which provides for various needs across a broad spectrum, including convenience) saves some time over mass transit, reduces scheduling complexity, and increases discretionary time.

And what is this "good time" to be used for? As an input to life style/identity consumption. In life style/identity consumption, time need not be "saved" as it was in convenience consumption; indeed, this type of time expenditure is to be *maximized*. But the process of time use must be enjoyable and engaging. "Good time" is to be mixed with services and goods to form enjoyable, stimulating, meaningful activity patterns, and the experience is to be prolonged as much as possible.

The stimulation component of life style/identity consumption is described by Scitovsky (1976). He summarizes the economic implications of the psychology of consumer satisfaction in a manner that clearly differentiates the need for stimulation from the need for comfort. Scitovsky correctly contrasts this search for *increased arousal* and tension with the implicit-need-satisfaction model of neo-classical economics, which holds that utility comes from *need reduction* (e.g., removal of the tension associated with unsatiated hunger). Scitovsky observes that even primitive tribes do not allocate their food efficiently in a series of equal-sized meals (the economically optimal allocation for need reduction). Instead, periods of near starvation are interspersed with "stimulating" feast days.

Since stimulation occurs when there are *dynamic changes* in the state of arousal (as long as extreme levels are avoided), attempting to maximize by merely reducing tension (i.e. yielding comfort) will ultimately prevent stimulation and bring about boredom.

The stimulation component of life style/identity consumption has also been described in a very pure form by Csikszentmihalyi (1975). Stimulation is a form of growth where new skills are learned in conjunction with exposure to challenging new situations. When challenges and skills are in the proper balance (called "flow" by Csikszentmihalyi), the possibility exists for creating a succession of "learning" increments (Karasek 1979, 1980c) in which the feeling of challenge and accomplishment alternate, providing the ever changing arousal levels (and avoiding extremes which lead to anxiety) required by the Scitovsky model of stimulation. Thus both new skills and new interest areas are characteristic of "utility" in life style/identity consumption.

The Contributions of Juster, Becker, and Linder. Working along somewhat different lines, Thomas Juster, Gary Becker, and Steffan B. Linder have underlined certain aspects of human behavior that need to be incorporated in even a preliminary sketch of the nature of consumption. Juster (1980) in his analysis of time budgets sees the individual as possessing two basic resources with which satisfactions are generated: time and "inherited wealth" (each person's stock of tangible capital, human capital, social networks, environmental amenities, and socio-political capital). Satisfactions flow out of the "process benefits" of activities that take place during both working and nonworking hours and are conditioned by "state of being," which is influenced by "inherited wealth."

Juster's studies indicate that process benefits vary widely in terms of the levels of satisfaction they generate. Some activities such as housework generate very low process benefits. Some, such as relating to peers, typically generate high benefits. There is also evidence that higher levels of satisfactions are generated by engaging in those things that one does well, so levels of acquired skill are important.

At least three implications for consumption theory arise out of these observations. The first is that consumers may be expected to value highly those goods or services that reduce the necessity for spending time in activities with low process benefits, and they will place a low value on goods or services that reduce the time spent on activities with high process benefits. Thus the consumer is likely to favor a good that reduces housework but will find uninteresting a service that reduces shopping time *if* he enjoys the personal contacts or the opportunities for comparing merchandise that characterize his trips to the market place.

A second implication is that the individual will value those goods or services that he feels contribute readily to the stock of "inherited wealth." Goods or services that serve to enhance one's acceptance in social relationships or that improve one's skills in activities (either work or play) for which the individual feels well suited may, for example, find special favor.

A third implication was voiced explicitly by Juster (1980): "People tend to have poorly developed preference functions for things they have not tried. Accordingly, the dynamics of change in preference functions will involve adaptive and learning processes."

Gary Becker (1980) has made major contributions to economic theory by carrying the traditional analysis of costs and benefits into the household economy. In particular, he has called attention to the rising value of people's time under

conditions of rising wages and noted the importance of producers' giving greater attention to time and place convenience
in designing products and services for the marketplace.

Steffan Linder (1970), working within the framework of
Becker's analysis, has examined in detail the implications of
the rising value of time. He notes that whereas under conditions of rising levels of income the ability to purchase goods is
open-ended, the time available to each individual is fixed. Yet
the consumption of more and more goods and services made
possible by rising income levels requires time — time for maintenance of goods and time for use and enjoyment. The individual is caught in a conflict in which time becomes increasingly scarce.

Linder's analysis is controversial, but there is clearly a major
contribution here for consumption theory: goods and services
that reduce maintenance or allow the maintenance burden to
be readily and inexpensively shifted are likely to be sought
after by consumers.

Evidence of Changing Patterns of Consumption. We know all too
little about the effects of income on consumption, and the data
available are poorly designed for its study. Categories of expenditures are essentially generic, providing incomplete evidence of the extent to which a given category of expenditure is
directed toward essential life-sustaining requirements, in contrast to more-discretionary preferences. Moreover, there is
the well-known demonstration effect, which may convert
"frills" into necessary components of consumption with rising
income and the passage of time.

Yet there is some tentative evidence that is highly sugges-
tive. Consumer Expenditures Survey materials of the Bureau
of Labor Statistics (1978) are available for two periods roughly
a decade apart (1961–1962 and 1971–1972). Based on a
large, stratified sample of households, they indicate the level
or expenditures for given types of consumption. In Table 2.1
we have classified expenditure categories under four headings: basic necessities, comfort/convenience, self identity–
life style, and automobile-related. (The latter is treated separately because it belongs to some extent in all three groups.)
While there may be some disagreement on classification of
individual categories, there would seem to be no question that

the classification scheme does provide, in general, a differentiation of more from less basic types of consumption.

The data strongly support the hypothesis that consumption
patterns are influenced by income. In 1972 – 1973, basic expenditures accounted for 62 percent of income spent in the
lowest income quintile versus 46 percent in the highest. Comfort expenditures are remarkably constant for comparisons
among income groups, while the portion spent on life style
purchases is 9 percent and 20 percent, respectively, for the
lowest and highest quintiles.

When 1972 – 1973 patterns are compared with those for
1961 – 1962 (reflecting changes during a period when per
capita incomes were rising sharply), we observe that shares of
expenditures for basic and comfort expenditure declined in
all income categories and rose for life style expenditures and
auto-related expenditures.

Particularly striking is the fact that the shift away from
basics was strong for both the low and high income groups.
Indeed, it seems to have been somewhat stronger for the
lowest income group than for the highest. There would seem
to be at least two factors contributing to this across-the-board
response. The first is that consumers of all levels seek some
measure of life style identification and accordingly mày direct
significant shares of incremental income toward such purchases, especially during a period of prosperity and rising
expectations. The second is simply that the categories of expenditures that are utilized in data gathering are of such
generality that they reflect only partially the true nature of
consumer behavior. Thus, in their expenditures for housing
and food (classified as basic) upper-income families may move
increasingly into gourmet dining and spend increasing
amounts on highly individualized home furnishings and
clothing as salaries and other receipts rise. Such spending is
not prompted by a search for fulfillment of basic requirements or even for greater comfort, but rather is a quest for
more fully realized life styles and self-identification.

A second piece of evidence relates not to income effects but
to possible new patterns of consumption. Table 2.2 shows that
between 1930 and 1960, Americans were heavily involved in
stocking up with time-saving appliances and automobiles to

Table 2.1 Shares of Consumer Expenditures by General Categories and Income Groups 1972–1973; and Changes in Shares between 1961–1962 and 1972–1973 (in percentages)

	$0–$3,000		$3,000–$7,000		$7,000–$12,000		$12,000–$20,000		$20,000 and over	
	shares	change in shares	shares	change in shares	shares	change in shares	shares	change in shares	shares	change in shares
Basic necessities	61.8	-7.2	56.6	-4.5	51.6	-5.6	48.9	-6.1	46.2	-3.7
Food at home	18.7	-7.7	17.9	-4.6	15.3	-5.6	14.0	-5.1	11.5	-3.9
House, shelter	22.9	5.1	17.7	3.5	16.0	3.2	14.1	2.5	13.9	3.4
House, utilities	6.8	-1.6	5.9	-0.1	5.0	-0.1	4.8	0.2	4.1	0.3
House, basic furnishings	1.8	-0.5	2.3	-0.6	2.4	-0.6	2.8	-0.3	3.1	0.1
Medical care	7.3	-0.8	7.6	-0.1	6.7	0.1	6.1	-0.3	5.7	-0.5
Clothing	4.4	-1.8	5.3	-2.6	6.2	-2.6	6.8	-3.0	7.8	-3.1
Comfort/Convenience	14.8	-1.2	14.8	-2.0	14.5	-1.9	14.1	-2.4	14.1	-3.5
Alcohol and tobacco	3.2	0.4	3.2	-0.7	3.3	-0.2	3.1	-0.3	2.7	-0.3
Personal care	2.0	-0.9	2.0	-1.1	2.0	-1.0	2.0	-0.8	2.0	-0.6
Laundry and dry cleaning	1.5	0.2	1.4	-0.1	1.2	-0.4	0.9	-0.7	0.9	-0.9
Household service and operations	6.5	1.4	6.1	1.2	5.3	0.5	5.2	0.3	5.3	-0.9
Appliances	1.0	-0.6	1.4	-0.3	1.7	-0.4	2.0	-0.3	2.1	-0.2
Miscellaneous (personal, business)	0.6	-0.7	0.7	-1.0	1.0	-0.4	1.0	-0.5	1.1	-0.8

Self identity/Life style	9.3	1.5	11.5	1.7	13.3	2.6	15.6	2.7	20.0	1.8
Leisure shelter	0.3	-0.1	0.4	0.0	0.5	-0.1	0.8	0.0	1.6	0.0
Food away from home	3.9	0.8	5.1	1.1	5.5	1.5	6.1	1.5	6.7	1.1
Leisure travel	1.2	0.3	1.4	0.4	1.7	0.8	2.2	0.9	3.3	0.1
Recreation purchases	3.1	1.0	3.8	0.7	4.4	0.8	4.9	0.6	5.4	0.6
Reading materials	0.5	-0.4	0.5	-0.3	0.6	-0.3	0.6	-0.3	0.6	-0.3
Education	0.3	-0.1	0.4	-0.1	0.6	-0.1	1.1	0.1	2.4	0.2
Automotive and others[a]	13.8	6.8	17.0	4.6	20.4	4.8	21.2	5.8	19.7	5.6
Total	100.0		100.0		100.0		100.0		100.0	

[a] Roughly 95 percent is auto related.

Note: Income groups for 1972–1973 are as indicated. In computing changes, income groups used for 1961–1962 are comparable after income levels have been adjusted for changes in consumer prices.

Source: Compiled from data in U.S. Department of Labor, Bureau of Labor Statistics, *Consumer Expenditures Surveys* for 1961–1962 and 1972–1973.

ease their burden of household chores and to accommodate themselves to the evolving automobile-oriented society, but that today we are approaching satiation in terms of levels of ownership. Of course, each new generation must equip itself with these basic goods, but we are no longer in an era in which the phenomenon of equipping a whole society with appliances and vehicles provides a major thrust to consumer demand.

There is little doubt that the forces that drove society toward mass adoption of these new goods were extremely strong. Lebergott (1967) notes that housework hours were reduced from an average of 12 to 5 per day from 1900 to 1966. The transformation in the allocation of time arising from the automobilization of our society is not readily expressed in any single statistic, but it was doubtless equally dramatic.

Factors of Change: Changing Social Environment

We do not argue that there are no new products with similar broad appeal just over the horizon. The recent rapid growth in microwave ovens and electronic toys indicates that the American public can still be attracted by innovative new devices. Much probably lies ahead for products that incorporate

---

Table 2.2   Percentage of Families with Electrical Appliances and Automobiles, 1912–1971

	1912	1932	1953	1971
Refrigerator	0	12	82	100
Range[a]	0	4	22	56
Dishwasher	0	1	3	26
Washing machine	0	27	70	92
Vacuum cleaner	0	30	54	92
Toaster	0	27	65	93
Coffee maker	0	19	47	89
TV	0	0	43	99
Automobile	1[b]	60[c]	75[d]	80
Percentage of mean mechanization	0	20	51	81

[a]Electric and gas.
[b]1910 figure.
[c]1930 figure.
[d]1960 figure.
Source: S. Lebergott, *The American Economy: Income, Wealth and Want* (Princeton: Princeton University Press, 1967), Tables 20 and 21.

sophisticated applications of the latest television, telephonic, and computer technology.

But it is probable that factors other than new products are now playing a more important role in changing the way in which the consumer spends his money. Such factors are to be found in the areas of urbanization, work, family structure, and social organization. The broad appeal of the automobile, appliances, and home furnishings of the fifties and sixties was strongly identified with an era in which middle America was moving into the suburbs and raising large families. In recent years new trends have emerged. Women are increasingly entering the workforce, marriages are occurring later, and the rate of reproduction has declined sharply. Moreover, the two-earner family is playing a larger role in the marketplace (bringing higher disposable incomes for an important segment of the population), and the proportion of older persons is increasing. All of these factors act to alter the composition of consumer demand. At the same time, the "golden age of suburbanization" — the years of rapid surburban growth — appears to be coming to an end *(New York Times,* March 16, 1980) as these areas enter a new era of aging facilities and higher costs. There is increasing evidence of both a move toward "gentrification," involving a return of at least a part of the middle class to the cities, and a new trend toward a growing importance of nonmetropolitan areas *(New York Times,* March 23, 1980).

Summing Up: Major Factors Influencing Consumption Patterns

At this point we have identified three sets of forces that impact patterns of consumption. The first is the tendency toward increased differentiation and proliferations of products and services that result from broader markets; the second is the tendency for the focus of consumption to shift, away from necessities and convenience goods and toward goods and services emphasizing life style and personal identity, as incomes rise. The third set of forces is environmental, involving changes in the family, urbanization, the nature of work, and the social milieu. These factors act together to influence consumption patterns.

Product differentiation takes place at all levels. Food, for example, no longer is offered in the marketplace as simple staples (flour, salt, basic meat cuts) but in packaged, branded form designed for particular (albeit often rather broad) market segments. These products are offered in forms suited to the needs of the housewife who must feed a family of six on a limited budget, the bachelor who intermittently prepares a "TV dinner," or the gourmet cook entertaining twelve.

But the constraint of income is ever present, limiting the ability of the consumer to move from necessity and comfort-oriented consumption to consumption involving patterns of behavior that emphasize development of life style and personal identity. At the same time the economic and social environment continuously impacts the marketplace. How people spend and organize their lives is conditioned by whether there are large or small families, whether or not women work, where people live and work, and a wide range of factors influencing the overall value system of society.

The Importance of Services in the Consumer Economy

The significance of services in consumption is implicit in the preceding analysis. Lancaster's demand theory provides the basic insight: if the consumer seeks multiple characteristics, then services and goods are likely to be complementary. Services may be consumed in combination with goods in order to acquire the desired mix of characteristics.

The importance of complementarity is readily observed. Goods may require maintenance or finance; frequently, they require special instruction, as in the case where learning to ski or to play tennis may involve a series of lessons from a professional instructor.

Greater emphasis on differentiation of products is likely to create additional demands for services. Delineating the product through market research, design, packaging, and advertising brings with it a new demand for producer-service inputs both in-house and out-of-house, a matter to be discussed in the chapter which follows. But product differentiation may also involve delivery of specific services to the customer himself as a part of the differentiated product package. Thus the seller may offer guarantees, maintenance contracts, financing, and even courses of instruction.

A somewhat different observation is that a shift toward patterns of consumption that emphasize self-realization and life style identification is likely to involve a greater reliance on services than obtains when consumption is focused on purchasing more basic, comfort-related goods. The customer will tend to look increasingly for a combination of characteristics that includes not only product performance and provision for repair, but also ease of finance, economizing of time, and, perhaps, opportunities to improve skills and to relate to others with similar interests.

There will be a greater need for services to tailor the package of goods and services to the customer's needs and purse. For the customer who desires to purchase only essential characteristics, the total "product" must be stripped down (e.g., only lift tickets at the ski slope and, perhaps, facilities for a lunchtime snack). For the customer who wishes all arrangements made, the "products" will involve a complex combination of goods and services that will include services of coordination: value can be added simply by making available at one time and place most or all of the complementary goods and services required (e.g., the traveler can secure at one place information, airline tickets, travelers checks, travel guides, hotel and auto reservations, and even arrangements for forwarding mail).

Implicit in all this is the increasing importance of the customer himself. Victor Fuchs (1968) has noted that cooperation of the purchaser is more important for services than for goods and is a major factor in determining productivity (e.g., a patient who gives an accurate medical history is likely to be more quickly and successfully treated).

But the point is more general. Where products are increasingly differentiated and numerous in the marketplace, or where the individual's special activities and life style become more important, the decisionmaking process becomes more complex and the consumer must be more directly involved. The institutional arrangements that are responsive to newly emerging needs will vary greatly. Some, such as the large

Table 2.3 Annual Rates of Change in Consumer Expenditures and Price Levels and Annual Shares of Consumer Expenditures by Major Types, Selected Periods and Years, 1948 to 1978 (in percentages)

Rates of change: consumer expenditures and price levels

	1948 to 1957	1957 to 1968	1968 to 1978
In current dollars			
Total goods	4.3	5.4	8.9
Durable goods	6.2 (1.5)	6.6 (1.2)	9.6 (4.1)
Nondurable goods	3.8 (1.2)	5.0 (1.8)	8.7 (6.1)
Services	7.5 (3.8)	7.1 (2.5)	10.6 (6.2)
Total expenditures	5.4	6.0	10.2
Disposable income	5.6	6.3	10.6
In 1972 dollars			
Total goods	3.0	3.5	3.3
Durable goods	4.6	5.4	5.2
Nondurable goods	1.3	4.1	2.4
Services	3.5	4.5	4.1
Total expenditures	3.2	3.9	3.6
Disposable income	3.4	4.9	3.0

Note: Annual rate of change in price levels is in parentheses.
Source: U.S. Department of Commerce, Bureau of Economic Analysis, *The National Income and Product Accounts of the U.S., 1929–74;* and *Survey of Current Business*, July 1979.

Shares: consumer expenditures			
1948	1957	1968	1978
68.4	62.2	57.9	54.1
13.1	14.0	14.9	14.8
55.3	48.2	43.0	39.3
31.6	37.8	42.1	45.9
100.0	100.0	100.0	100.0
60.2	59.0	56.6	54.4
10.6	12.0	14.0	16.3
49.6	47.0	42.6	38.1
39.8	41.0	43.4	45.6
100.0	100.0	100.0	100.0

supermarket and variety store, have evolved by recognizing the importance of affording the customer an opportunity to examine a wide variety of merchandise. They offer less, not more services. But others, such as the modern airline, hotel, travel agent, real estate agent, investment house, insurance agent, or bank, reach out to the customer and seek to work directly with him or her to identify and fill specific requirements.

The share of personal consumption expenditures accounted for by services has risen continuously since World War II, although much of this rise has been due to the disproportionate increase in prices of services (Table 2.3). Stated briefly, the postwar experience is one in which the services share (in current dollars) advanced sharply, from the immediate postwar period through 1957, from 31.6 to 37.8 percent, and then grew consistently, but more slowly, through 1978, to account for roughly 46 percent today.

This account is changed somewhat by deflation. Expenditures for durables, when measured in constant dollars, grew more rapidly than services in each period.

There is at least one indication, however, that the importance of consumer services as revealed by the data may be understated. Such evidence is found in the rapid, recent growth of retail employment. In spite of the marked shift toward self-service in grocery, drug, variety, and even department stores, retailing's share of total employment increased during the seventies. One explanation is that employment growth has been most rapid in those outlets, such as specialty shops, that cater to the individual needs of the customer, providing advice or some measure of service in addition to simply displaying merchandise and making the sale. The detailed data presented in Table 2.4 give some support to this hypothesis.

Yet consumer spending still remains essentially goods-oriented. Not only does life for many seem to revolve around the automobile, but there is a strong tendency to equip oneself heavily for each new activity, especially for leisure activities. The dramatic increase in the popularity of boating has brought with it not only the purchase of boats, but also a formidable array of gear, including special attire. The new tennis devotee requires racquets, balls, clothing, and even

Table 2.4   Retail Outlets with Annual Rates of Employment Growth in Excess of That for All Retailing, 1972 to 1978

	Annual growth rates (percentage)
Retail nurseries and garden stores	6.3
Other food stores	5.7
Auto and home supply stores	5.1
Family clothing stores	4.4
Furriers and miscellaneous apparel and accessory stores	3.7
Radio, television, and music stores	6.8
Eating and drinking places	6.9
Used merchandise stores (including antiques)	6.4
Miscellaneous shopping goods stores	6.3
All retail outlets	3.5

Source: Harold Goldstein, "Recent Structural Changes in Employment in the United States," 1980.

unique luggage. Additional examples can be supplied almost endlessly. No wonder a colleaue of the writer's was prompted to remark, "We Americans like to take our services out in goods!"

What then is the relationship of goods to services? Is it complementary or is it competitive? The answer is that it is both, for there are contradictory forces at work. On one hand there is the thrust of the changing nature of consumption which, as we have seen, creates new needs for the "binding" functions of services (information, training, coordination, time-economizing, and the like). On the other, there are forces that tend to restrict the purchase of services and to favor the purchase of goods.

The first of these latter forces is the tendency for prices to rise more rapidly for consumer services than for goods, at least when the latter are mass produced. The price of a basic electric hand drill for use in the workshop costs no more today than a quarter-century ago, yet the services of a caddy at the local golf club have probably risen several times. The example probably overstates the case, but more representative ones can as readily be suggested. The relative cheapness and quality of our durables are hallmarks of our modern economy — a major result of our accumulation of capital and technology.

Although the popular notion that services are unproductive is invalid, there is an important core of truth to William Baumol's contention (1967) that services tend to be susceptible to a chronic "cost disease." He argues that wage increases in services follow those in industries where technology and capital inputs increase output per worker, but that similar gains in productivity do not occur in services. The result is a disproportionate rise in costs and prices in services.

This is not true for all consumer services, and it it likely to be less true in the future as services are increasingly "industrialized." Yet it is undeniable that most consumer services have shown more rapid rises in price than most consumer goods (Table 2.3).

A second force making for tendencies to economize on services is the increasing cost of buying certain services in the market relative to "doing it yourself." Here the impetus is the impact of rising tax rates on the value of services performed in the home. As inflation drives dollar income levels into higher tax brackets without commensurately increasing real income, the customer saves increasingly more by performing the service "in-house." At the same time he finds, increasingly, that the needed goods are readily available in convenient form and with necessary instructions, manuals, etc. Anyone who stands in a weekend checkout line at Sears will observe a constant stream of customers awaiting their turn to purchase a variety of equipment and supplies for repair and maintenance of autos and for household renovations.

One can raise the objection that the trend toward "do it yourself" does not square with the tendency for people to regard their time as increasingly scarce. Yet both conditions do seem to occur together in our modern life. It is likely that the explanation of the apparent contradiction lies in Juster's observations regarding process benefits. The consumer may find it desirable to perform certain services "in-house" when there is a sense of attainment associated with mastering of basic manual skills, yet find time too scarce for activities with low or negative process benefits, such as preparing income tax returns. He may also find time less scarce under certain conditions (an uncommitted weekend at home) than under others (a long-awaited vacation or the harried days that immediately precede it).

Summary and Implications

Clearly one should expect the complementarity between goods and services to remain a major dimension of consumption. Moreover, the forces identified in this chapter should continue to push in the direction of greater product differentiation as long as developments in the labor markets (to be examined in Chapter 4), which continue to make for a relatively greater segmentation of earnings among workers, contribute to a continuing need to adjust consumer products to a wide spectrum of income and purchasing power. In short, all these trends are likely to make for continuity of the tendencies toward short product lives, frequent product modification, and an emphasis on targeting specific consumer markets.

Notes

[1] This is a central thesis of Alvin Toffler's *Future Shock* (1970). Several of the examples cited below are drawn from this work.

[2] The special financial problems that derive from course proliferation in the modern university have been analyzed by Ernest Bloch (1977).

[3] Toffler (1970), op. cit., p. 266.

3. Changing Markets, Changing Firms, and the Rise of Producer Services

This chapter deals with the major transformations at work in the way we produce. Attention is directed not so much to the increased application of capital and technology to production processes within the plant, which is fundamental and well recognized, but to changes in organizational and institutional arrangements of the private sector: to the growth in size and importance of large corporations, to the shift toward more complex and advanced managerial structures, and to the growth of producer services. It is important to recognize at the outset that the processes involved are not only complex and cumulative but that they are highly interactive.

The paragraphs to follow highlight some key aspects of the transformation that has been at work.

The Rising Importance of Planning, Developmental, and Administrative Functions

For the past two hundred years, the processes of physical transformation — transformation of material, especially in manufacturing — have lent themselves most readily to application of physical capital and to the incorporation of new, science-based technology. Accordingly, there has been a marked tendency to substitute high technology – embodied capital for labor in goods-producing processes. In turn, this tendency has gradually acted to shift management's attention away from the plant, where processes are increasingly routinized and costs brought under control, toward other areas which previously had been regarded as deserving of only secondary priority. Thus attention has shifted to activities that involve planning, product development, market strategy, and administrative control.

If the improvement of productive processes within the plant have made possible such a shift in focus, the increasing complexity of the management task has made it imperative. We observed in Chapter 2 how the broadening of the market brought with it increasing product differentiation, segmentation of markets, and the need for product innovation in consumer goods and services. It has brought similar developments in the marketplace for investment goods and intermediate products. As the number of potential business customers has increased, it has become worthwhile for firms to design equipment and supplies to meet the special operating needs of different segments of the industrial market. Thus, in all markets, whether final or intermediate, the seller must reach out to the customer and tailor the product or service to his needs. He must innovate; he must promote; he must serve. All this requires increased attention to research and development, to market strategy (what segments of the market to target, how to price, how to advertise, how to distribute, how to manage relationships with dealers, etc.), and to planning (at what point to bring out new products, when and to what extent to move into new domestic and international markets).

In addition, other functions have come to require far greater emphasis than in an earlier era. Larger firm size and the development of financial markets have brought new needs for financial expertise. The growth of government regulation has increased the difficulty of working within the regulatory framework, made necessary continuous interaction with public sector agencies, and increased the need to make the firm's position known both to government and to the public through explicit public relations tactics and through trade associations.

Finally, with growth in firm size, new emphasis has been directed toward the internal management of the firm itself. On the one hand, there is a new emphasis on coordination and control of costs, both at the plant level and within the expanding administrative-planning structure. On the other, there is a rising need for attention to recruitment, training programs, salary and promotion policy, pension plans, and a variety of other fringe benefits.

Almost any of these activities may be undertaken either inside or outside the firm. Manufacturers, for example, may make use of in-house corporate counsel or hire the services of an outside firm; they may plan new marketing strategy within the organization or make use of an advertising agency or market research consultant. The list of options may be extended almost indefinitely to include such diverse activities as engineering, R and D, janitorial services, pension plan management, counseling of employees, and even the hiring and firing of executives.

Evidence of a rapid growth in producer-service-like activities, carried on in-house and similar to that observed for independent producer-services firms in Chapter 1, is presented in Table 3.1. It indicates that nonproduction workers in manufacturing have increased as a share of employment in manufacturing establishments from 23 percent to 25 percent from 1954 to 1978, growing at an annual rate of 1.3 percent during a period in which production workers declined. Employment in central administrative offices and auxiliary establishments (CAO & A) is seen to have grown at a far more rapid rate of 6 percent per annum — not unlike the growth

---

Table 3.1 Rates of Change and Distribution of Employment: Production Workers, Nonproduction Workers, CAO&A Employees in Manufacturing, 1954–1978

	Annual rate of growth	Shares	
	1954–1978	1954	1978
Manufacturing	0.9	100.00	100.00
Production workers	-0.5	76.85	69.39
Nonproduction workers	1.3	20.33	24.45
CAO&A employees[a]	6.0	2.82	6.20

[a]CAO&A employment is reported only where administrative personnel are located in separate physical facilities. Accordingly, there is a serious underreporting in CAO&A employment. Administrative employment not reported as CAO&A is reported as nonproduction workers. The abbreviated classifiation CAO&A refers to central administrative offices and auxiliaries.
Source: U.S. Department of Commerce, *Annual Survey of Manufacturers* 1978 and *Census of Manufacturing* 1958.

observed among the producer-service firms (4.5 percent per annum).

Growth of Markets, Growth of Firms, and the Rise of Producer Services

Stigler's Pioneer Analysis of the Rise of Producer Service Firms; The Importance of Market and Firm Size. One of the most fundamental insights in economics is Adam Smith's dictum that "the division of labor is limited by the extent of the market." In a classic article, George Stigler (1951) demonstrated how this principle applies to the growth of firms that supply intermediate goods and services to user firms. Stigler called attention to the fact that a firm's production is the result of performing a number of functions, each having its own set of costs, which are likely to behave differently from the others with increases in output. Where production costs for a given function are subject to increasing economies of scale, a broadening of the market will at some point make it feasible for a specialist firm or firms to enter the marketplace and provide the good or service on favorable terms. Thus increasing size of markets makes for "pecuniary economies" in the form of efficient, outside sources of goods or services.

But growth in overall size of market provides only a partial explanation of the remarkable growth in producer services. A fuller explanation requires recognition of the importance of the rise of the large modern corporation and the increasing burden of administrative and developmental functions suggested above. These developments provide new and urgent demands for specialization of producer services: first within firms, and then, as demands rise past some threshold, for the development of firms selling producer services on the open (external) market. The logic of this process highlights one of the fundamental roles of producer services — that of integrating or "binding" together the increasingly differentiated, specialized parts and functions of the market system. Indeed, from the standpoint of the system as a whole, the increasing role of government can be partly seen in the same light: as providing a variety of systemwide, producer-service-like functions — those which create and maintain the physical, informational, and political networks needed to integrate an increasingly complex economic system

Factors Acting to Increase Market and Firm Size. A theory of firm growth needs to deal with the interaction between market size and firm size. Increasing market size has the effect of increasing firm size, as long as there are economies of scale to be exploited. Conversely, increasing firm size, to the extent that it permits exploitation of economies of scale and the integration of otherwise separated markets, leads to increasing market size as firms reach out to establish distribution systems and promote their products over even broader areas. The key mediating factor here is economies of scale.

We will not dwell on the issue of the forces that have contributed to an increase in market size, since many of them have already been analyzed in Chapter 2. Suffice it to say that on the demand side, rising income and changing consumer taste and behavior have pushed the limits of the market to new levels. On the supply side, firms have acted (1) to transform the consumer goods market, (2) to open up new markets by introducing products and services that were previously provided outside the market arena (e.g., prepared meals, entertainment, income tax preparation), and (3) to reach out to new consumers by moving abroad. All of these initiatives have contributed to broadening the market in ways that would have been almost inconceivable thirty or forty years ago.

Yet this ability by firms both to contribute to and to benefit from this broadening of the market materialized only because of accompanying structural transformations of the firm of the type analyzed by Chandler (1977).

Changing Economics of Scale: The Shift from the Plant Level to the Firm Level. Traditionally, economies of scale have been associated with the technology of goods production, that is, with the ability to force down the cost of manufactured units through increases in production runs at higher levels of utilization of fixed capital (plant or equipment). This concept of scale economies based on goods production has become too narrow a view. Under the most modern conditions of production, economies of scale at the *plant* or *establishment* level no longer stand as a barrier to corporate size, having been replaced by economies of scale at the *firm* level: economies in the "higher-level" developmental, financial, and administrative functions of the firm. This calls for greater specialization of service functions, enabling firms to manage the increasing differentiation of products and the extension of product lines, to link markets and establishments through improved distribution and communications, to revamp the organizational structure of multi-unit, multi-staged operations, and to anticipate change in different but related markets.

This shift of managerial emphasis from the establishment to the firm level has meant a substantial transformation in retail and consumer service delivery and has permitted the growth of large new firms or of large divisions within established firms. Firms have been able to shift the performance of functions of inventory control, purchasing, advertising, promotion of brand names and trade mark, and long-term financing to the level of overhead offices, while restricting the functions of establishments to the delivery of the main line service itself. Thus, they have been able to capitalize on substantial economies of scale and turn businesses, once left to small local entrepreneurs, into large, multi-establishment enterprises. Indeed, as Chandler pointed out (1977), Sears understood this principle long ago.

What is new, however, is the extent to which this way of operating has been applied in the recent decades to numerous lines of services: hotels (Hilton, Holiday Inn, Sheraton), restaurants (McDonald, Burger King, Wendy's), car repair (Midas, AAMCO), movie theaters (Loews, Gulf and Western), car rental (Avis, Hertz, National), residential real estate brokers (Century 21, ERA, Realty World), or even funeral parlors (SCI) *(Wall Street Journal,* December 6, 1979). New ways of internalizing potential scale economies have been found through standardization of previously highly personalized services (standardization of outputs), through standardization of the service delivery process (standardization of the production process), and through the introduction of computer technology to link the establishment to the central office.[1] At the same time, other forces have acted on the demand side to broaden these markets such as, for instance, more demand for travel on the part of businessmen and increasing participation of women in the labor force, which favors the growth of food establishments.

It is important to emphasize the cumulative nature of these processes. Just as physical capital has increased and production technology has improved through a complex process made possible by yearly increments of net investment, by scientific advancement, and by industrial research, so has management's capability to manage large organizations increased through a cumulative process. A host of new techniques, such as inventory control, market analysis, product testing, cash budgeting, financial control, and capital investment analysis, have been developed, disseminated quickly and widely, and become a part of an increasing body of managerial "technology." The level of general education has improved continuously as has the level of professional training for business, creating human capital which embodies the new managerial "technology." Increasingly, corporations find it possible to put together skilled teams to find ways of overcoming previous managerial constraints upon the size of firm and of innovating, financing, and promoting new products.

Size and Growth of Firms as a Basis for New Demand for Producer Services: Maintenance versus Development. A problem with dealing analytically with the significance of firm size is that "size" is less a variable than a concept, qualitative and multidimensional in nature (Georgescu-Roegen 1972, p. 105). A major concern is how the supply and demand for various services are influenced by the evolving structure of production. Structural attributes of the firm include its size, the geography of its markets, the degree of diversification and other characteristics of its products (durability, standardization, etc.), its age, and its organization (Caves 1980). Size expressed in terms of a single measure (employment, assets, or sales) is useful because several important structural indicators correlate with size reasonably well, but at some point it is necessary to penetrate the veil of "size."

It is important to distinguish a firm's "being" a certain size from its "becoming" a certain size. In other words, there are both static and dynamic considerations in discussing the firm's demand for services. Some services may be demanded principally to deal with the consequences of size, others are utilized mainly to attain a larger size. Here we encounter the distinction between *systems maintenance* and *systems development*, discussed below.

Thus large firms need certain functions to be carried out in a more specialized way than do smaller firms. These functions include management, communication and control functions, employee screening, selection and evaluation, employee training, contract negotiation, and marketing. Service functions that become increasingly important where the firm is dealing with forces of change include product development, research, strategic planning, and development of new sources of funds, either external or internal. These latter functions are also likely to be more specialized the larger the size of the firm. An important generalization suggested by case studies of selected corporations is that integrative functions become increasingly important as the firm becomes larger and attempts to diversify (Cohen et al., 1980).

One way in which services are important in coping with change involves the firm's efforts to deal with the product cycle. Product markets become saturated as new markets are penetrated and as products become standardized elements in either producer or consumer budgets. In order to expand, firms operating in such markets must then choose an appropriate strategy or combination of strategies: (1) differentiate existing products or services; (2) develop new products or services; (3) offer more services with existing goods; and/or (4) develop new technologies. The genesis and implementation of these strategies is described in the case studies by Cohen et al. cited above (1980). These product cycle considerations highlight the increasing importance of services in the processes of development or adaptation at the level of the firm, services that include, for instance, design, R & D, marketing, or advertising. An effective linkage between the firm's production, product development, and marketing efforts is required to carry out the firm's strategy. Strategic bundles of services are not only used to differentiate products and improve customer loyalty, but also to help raise barriers to entry into a firm's product line.

Transactions and Adjustment Costs. In the broadest sense, the firm in coping with change is coping largely with uncertainty. The services implicated are those that put the firm in a better position to make unprogrammed adaptations, achieve some control over its environment, and influence its future. They include advertising and public relations, strategic planning, research, forecasting, product innovation, management consulting services which assist the adaptation of the firm, financial service innovations which assist the formation of new ventures or which facilitate the reduction of risks or transaction costs, and, nowadays, even liaison/lobbying services which deal with various levels of government.

These services relate directly to what are referred to in the economic literature as *transactions costs* and *adjustment costs*. Transactions costs are the costs of bringing the two (supply and demand) sides of a market together. Adjustment costs are the costs of increasing the supply of those resources whose production takes significant lengths of time: resources with a long gestation period such as highly skilled or educated labor, sophisticated machinery, entrepreneurship, or organization.

Recent work by Oliver Williamson (1980) provides a detailed classification and analysis of transactions costs. The implications of his analysis for understanding producer services are extremely important but have yet to be realized. First, almost every type of transactions cost identified by Williamson has its counterpart in a specialized producer service. Second, specialization of producer services for external markets may influence industrial organization. Third and conversely, changes in industrial organization will affect the demand for specialized producer services. Accordingly, those factors that affect firms' transactions costs will affect the growth of producer services. They include uncertainty, complexity, asymmetrical distributions of information, and problems of incentives, control, and coordination in business enterprise.

The question of how transactions costs and adjustment costs vary with firm size and rate of growth is, therefore, an important issue to explore if we are to understand the growth of producer services. Empirical work needs to identify services provided within firms and to examine intrafirm elasticities of demand. Very little has been done in this area, in part because the data problems are severe. "Program-budgets" that detail firm expenditures in several functional service areas would be required. Some services, such as management consulting, can serve several functional areas. Literature on the size and growth of both organisms and organizations indicates that simple algometric rules seldom apply. The liver does not grow at the same rate as the brain, and neither grow at the same rate as the body as a whole. Similar remarks could be made about the personnel department and corporate headquarters in relation to firm size. The "demand" (or growth) elasticities for various service functions at the firm level may vary widely. In fact, the elementary economic distinction between "need" and "demand" will have to be made here, too. Even though there may be demonstrable "needs" for producer services by firms of various sizes, one should expect variation in the extent which firms with similar characteristics have elected to spend for services and the extent to which those services are specialized.

Some tentative hypotheses for empirical testing can be offered. First, the distinction between firms being a certain size and becoming a certain size should have empirical content. Since many other types of economic organization beside private business firms are source of demand for producer services, the distinction can be generalized and rephrased as services for *system maintenance* versus those for *system development*. Also, at this point demand is simply viewed as firms' expenditures of money or time on service functions, without any distinction as yet between in-house provision or purchases of services on external markets. The demand for services assisting system maintenance should increase cross-sectionally with system size. Services assisting system development should expand, over time, as a function of firms' growth rates, the uncertainty of their economic environment, and the extent of firms' diversification into new market and product areas. The growth and diversification of producer services serving both purposes, such as management consulting, accounting, and legal services, should be statistically sensitive to all these factors; but the "leading edge" (fastest growing activities within these industries) should be those oriented to the development of business systems.

Furthermore, one would expect to observe thresholds of firm demand for producer services, just as one observes service thresholds by city size. The more specialized or more "advanced" the service, the more likely it is to be demanded by larger firms. Below a certain firm size, very little demand should be observed. Empirically, the threshold should be observed as a sharp discontinuity in plots of firms' expenditures for producer services versus firm size. The thresholds for maintenance of in-house service functions should be significantly higher. A certain scale or frequency of demand for legal services, for example, will be required before a corporation can justify the maintenance of in-house legal staff. Even then, more specialized, intermittent service needs are likely to be met externally. This leads into the following area of concern.

In-House versus Out-of-House Producer Services: The Decision "to Make or Buy"

In this context, another issue of business strategy comes into focus: should the firm "make" or "buy" producer services? Stigler (1951) cites two major factors influencing this choice: complementarity and economies of scale.

Complementarity. Complementarity refers to the extent to which service functions can be provided internally without raising the firm's costs of carrying out other functions; i.e. without competing with other functions for existing scarce resources within the firm. Complementarity exists if services can be provided largely as a joint product, enabling better utilization of managerial or other scarce resources. Services are more likely to be provided internally to the extent they are complementary, and to be provided externally to the extent that they are "rival" (Stigler 1951).

Williamson's work on transaction costs helps to go beyond Stigler in elucidating the concept of complementarity. A producer service may (or should) be internalized to the extent that it enables the firm to build firm-specific human capital or to make better use of such resources. Moreover, services are more likely to be internalized to the extent that they involve transactions that are specific to the firm and its particular resources, because the transactions are fraught with complexity or ambiguity, involve "first mover" advantages, or involve resources which are highly specialized. For example, transactions involving new product innovation, strategic considerations, or firm-specific information would be implicated. The latter, in turn, implicate some of the most important and fastest growing among producer services functions: research and development, marketing, strategic planning, information processing, and personnel services.

Economies of Scale. To imply that a firm should internalize complementary service functions, however, is not to imply that a firm *can* do so. Keeping specialized service personnel on the firm's payroll may be justified only if the firm attains a certain size or scale of operations. Nor is it necessarily true that, if a firm should externalize a "rival" service function, this will be possible.

Stigler's line of reasoning was that the increasing size of markets would increase both specialization and the realization of potential economies of scale. What was not made clear is that specialization is prior to the realization of economies of scale. In the case of producer services, newly specialized service functions arose first within firms. "Needs" for new service functions arose with increasing size (and various correlates of size such as complexity, geographic scope, and diversification). Whether service "needs" were translated into "demands" (i.e., budgeted allocations for specialized service personnel) depended, again, on the size of the firm, because the frequency with which the need arose was a major factor in determining whether or not resources would be allocated.

Initially, only the largest firms could justify the maintenance of specialized services personnel. But in time, increasing specialization of services functions within the larger firms signaled to entrepreneurs both within and outside the firm that there were new markets to be exploited. Gradually, a specialized producer services industry was created through entrepreneurship. This in turn made it possible for smaller firms, those with more intermittent services needs, to have access to specialized services.

Once established on external markets, the producer services industry began to develop with a dynamic that is common to most other industries. Some flavor of this dynamic was first intimated by Greenfield (1966). Increasingly specialized resources, both human and physical, were created to meet the requirements of the new, growing industry. In an environment of growth and competition, services output became increasingly specialized, and many of the original specializations became gradually more routinized and standardized functions.

It is these latter developments over time — specialization of inputs and standardization of the (older) outputs — that gave rise to economies of scale. This is demonstrated in several examples by Greenfield that contradict Stigler's earlier intuition. Specialization rather than economies of scale must be seen as the driving force for externalization. Only later in the development process of the market for producer services do scale economies become a precondition for extending the market to firms that otherwise would have been unable to purchase such services (by bringing prices down).

Note here a spatial, locational dimension of the in-house/ out-of-house decision. Specialization and diversification of economic activities tend to be greater in more dense urban locations (Lampard 1955). Thus, one can hypothesize that tendencies to externalization will be greater with increased urbanization, that is, with increases in city size. This hypothesis is consistent with certain observations on the spatial localization and diffusion of business services made by Bearse (1977), but as will be shown in Chapter 5, the relationship between city size and the role of producer services is by no means a simple and straightforward one.

The misconception, implicit in Stigler's original treatment, is to confuse economies of scale with frequency of demand. Large firm size is a necessary (though not sufficient) prerequisite for internalization, because there must exist a certain minimum frequency of demand to justify specialization within the firm. Once the services functions have become available externally, however, the link between demand frequency and specialization is broken, since service specializations are now supplied independent of firm size of the user. In fact, the development of specialized producer services industries as we know them is contingent upon the identification and aggregation of many intermittent sources of demand. These sources will include the demand for specialized "complementary" services by firms that cannot justify creation of an in-house capability.

The Influence of the Regulatory Environment. Finally, it is important to recognize that the strong tendency for externalization of producer services may be contradicted by forces no less powerful that bear on the environment of producer-service delivery. The regulatory framework under which the producer-service industry must operate is one such example. For example, many have already observed the recent tendency among large nonfinancial firms to re-internalize part of their financing function, either through the takeover of insurance companies or through the internal development of large consumer credit divisions. A quick reading of this situation shows that today close to half of the Fortune 500 firms control either an insurance company or a consumer credit facility (*Directory of Corporate Affiliations* 1978). In addition, it is well known that the amount of lending between cash-rich and cash-poor nonfinancial corporations has dramatically increased, at the expense of transactions previously handled between financial and nonfinancial firms. It is usually agreed upon that this development has come about largely as a result of the increasing cost of borrowing from financial institutions — a cost that in many ways reflects the burden of regulation.

Since this subject has been taken at least a few steps beyond Stigler, it is important to note outstanding areas of inquiry. First, although economies of scale in services provision are clearly implicated theoretically (and suggested by some data), attempts to measure economies of scale in producer services are rare, mainly limited to financial services and public utilities. Much empirical work needs to be done.

Second, future research needs to go beyond measures of "size" to address in detail the significance of structural attributes of firms. Does it make any difference to the make-vs.-buy decision how the firm is organized, how its workforce is managed, and so forth? Case studies can provide some preliminary insights, but the analysis will have to be extended to a larger statistical base to allow generalization.

Third, one needs to research more carefully the influence of the legal and regulatory environment on the development of producer services. Fourth, one needs to determine how sensitive are tendencies of internalization/externalization to the emerging competitive structure of producer-services industries themselves. Other questions might be added to this list, but these are some of the major items for a research agenda.

Human Capital and Producer Services

As Gary Becker has pointed out (1980), the two real forms of economic capital– physical (goods) capital and human (knowledge) capital — are not substitutes but complements. Thus, the increasing human capital intensity of industry is itself a major driving force in the economic transformation. This is indicated by a services transformation within manufacturing itself, where the proportion of nonproduction workers has been rising rapidly and steadily for many years. Increasing human capital intensity of the labor force has been driven, too, by the broadening and deepening of the educational infrastructure and the growth of learning.

These developments pose challenges and opportunities for the firm. The challenge is to provide better management of human resources. The opportunity is for improved utilization of the firm's professional and technical personnel, especially insofar as it provides a logical avenue of diversification into services as a part of the product line. The converse also holds: diversification into services enables more effective utilization of relatively fixed human resources.

Thus, there is a corollary, interactive development of producer services and producer-services personnel. This is a positive feature of any young, dynamic, growing sector of the economy. Yet this feature must not be allowed to obscure some real and perhaps troublesome human resource issues in the growth of the services economy. One danger is that the economic transformation will aggravate tendencies toward stratification of the labor force. While the mobility and human capital of some of those working in producer-service occupations will be enhanced, those of other segments of the labor force, notably production workers and consumer-service workers, may be diminished. These issues are discussed in Chapter 4.

New Opportunities for Small Firms

Paradoxically, the developments discussed above have favored both large firms and small. The necessity of reaching large markets has provided opportunities for large corporations to play even larger roles. Their increasing mastery over many problems associated with product differentiation and promotion and their refinement of techniques to deal with their internal bureaucracy have permitted them to dominate many markets. But these very developments have at the same time created opportunities for small firms. The economics of out-of-house production of highly specialized producer services is such that many of these services can be supplied by a handful of professionals and their limited staffs. At the same time, in the consumer marketplace a new emphasis on highly differentiated, customer-oriented products and services has created new niches for small specialty shops and service firms. These firms find it easier to establish themselves in an environment in which increased availability of producer services makes it possible to "farm out" a number of basic functions, such as accounting, legal and pension work, and the procurement of personnel.

It appears, therefore, that the transformation of the U. S. economy is mixed with respect to firm size. On the one hand, it would be inappropriate to infer, as Fuchs did in his early work, *The Services Economy,* that domination of the economy by large corporate units would tend to diminish. Neither can one infer that there will be a major resurgence of small buiness or, on the other hand, a continued secular decline of small business entrepreneurship. The transformation should help to renew somewhat the springs of entrepreneurship and maintain the vitality of the small business sector in the U. S. economy, even while the skewness of the firm size distribution and economic concentration continue to increase. These are not inconsistent developments. As Sylos-Labini (1957) and other students of industrial organization recognize, corporate oligopolies provide an "umbrella" under which a variety of small businesses can continue to exist, including, presumably, a variety of producer services.

The Role of the New Technology

Although we have not undertaken to examine in detail the impact of new microprocessor technology on the changing structure and mode of operation of modern business, it is obviously a factor of paramount importance. Like the shift to the use of electricity and the introduction of the telephone, the application of the computer has diffused into every aspect of the operation of the private and public sectors. The impact, moreover, appears to be still in its infancy.

A striking aspect of the new technology is that it seems to be particularly useful in its application to nonproduction activities, largely at the firm level, whereas most technological advances of the past have tended to focus on production activities within the plant. These applications, which feature the use of the computer, often coupled with the telephone and xerography, have impacted office and administrative activities at every level. An interaction is taking place between scientific advances, the development of human capital, and the perfection of new "white collar" technology, including a host of new techniques such as inventory control, market potential analysis, and a wide range of developments falling under the general headings "word processing" and "communications." Throughout the economy the level of general education has improved, as has the level of professional training for business, creating human capital that embodies the new technology. Yet it is the combination of steady decreases in cost and increase in capabilities of this new equipment that stands as the overriding factor that makes these new techniques possible and drives management forward to ever more sophisticated applications. The new technology and its applications have largely to do with processing and provision of information. One can predict that those producer-services firms and occupations that are information-oriented will be among the fastest growing services activities.

Summary and Implications

This chapter indicates how many of the most important and fascinating features of the transformation of the U. S.

economy are revealed by a focus on producer services, a part of the services sector whose significance has been generally overlooked. Since these are overwhelmingly intermediate services rather than services sold to final demand, their role in the transformation of the business firms, in productivity, and in the spatial organization of the late 20th century U. S. economy needs much more attention than it has yet received.

Notes

[1]Standardization of production and of the product have been dealt with extensively by Theodore Levitt, who describes the process as "industrialization of the services" (Levitt 1977).

4. Employment: Occupational and Earnings Structures and the Changing Nature of Work

Moses Abramovitz (1972) has observed that the transformation in employment, which has characterized our time, is largely a shift from "hard-handed" to "soft-handed" work — from jobs calling for relatively low inputs of human capital which were filled largely by men, to jobs with higher demands on education and training, which can be filled by men and women. This transformation reflects in large measure the two great transformations we have already discussed. It involves the transformation in what we produce — the shift in composition of final demand, under conditions of rising incomes, toward a rising importance of health and educational services, of public sector social and regulatory services, and of consumer services. It involves also the transformation in how we produce — the ways in which both the private and public sectors have responded to the requirements of expanding markets, advancing technology, and changing tastes by increases in specialization, and shifting of emphasis toward coordination, planning, and innovation.

But it involves as well significant differentials in rates of improvement of productivity — or more accurately in the

The analysis of the service workforce in this chapter is based largely on materials developed by Marcia Freedman (1976, 1980). We are indebted to Dr. Freedman for making her worksheets available to us.

rates of substitution of technology-embodied capital for labor — in the goods-producing and -handling activities relative to many of the services.

Accordingly, the examination of employment trends within industrial grouping in Chapter 1 (Table 1.2) provides only a first approximation of what has occurred in employment. Yet it is a valuable first approximation, for it shows clearly how, with the decline in agricultural employment and in the share of employment accounted for by manufacturing jobs, the services have become increasingly important. It shows also that the growth of employment has not proceeded uniformly in all industrial groupings.

It is against the background of these industrial changes that changes in the occupations and earnings composition of the workforce must be examined and some assessment made of the impact of the rise of services on employment. Industries differ widely in terms of occupational composition and the earnings levels that characterize them. The transformation of employment that has occurred has involved a complex process by which occupations have shifted in importance, in large measure as a result of varying industrial trends.

The purpose of this chapter is twofold: first, to examine the occupational and earnings composition and other key employment characteristics of the several main groups of services, and second, to observe the changes in employment within these groups, not simply in terms of numbers of jobs but also in terms of occupations, earnings, and underlying characteristics of work.

Structure and Change: Occupational and Earnings Characteristics

Occupational-Earnings Composition. Taken as a whole, services are indeed more "soft-handed" than goods-producing activities. They have a higher percentage of white collar employment (professional, technical, managerial, clerical, and sales) and jobs in the "service worker" category than do the goods-producing activities, 63 and 19 percent versus 35 and 1 percent, respectively (Table 4.1)[1]

The service industries are by no means homogeneous in terms of occupational composition, however (Table 4.1). Pro-

Table 4.1 Occupational Shares of Employment within Industries, Total Services, Total Nonservices and All Industries; Average Earnings (000s omitted) and Rank for Industry-Occupation Cells, 1975[a]

	Professionals	Technicians	Managers	Office clericals	Nonoffice clericals	Sales	Craftsmen	Operatives	Service workers	Laborers	Average Rank
Manfacturing (%)	5.4	5.2	11.5	6.2	5.1	2.8	14.9	42.2	1.9	5.0	
$Earning/Rank	17.4(3)	14.1(2)	16.1(1)	7.5(2)	8.8(3)	8.8(3)	11.2(2)	7.5(3)	7.2(2)	5.0(1)	2.2
Distributive services (%)	3.3	3.4	17.0	9.6	11.6	9.5	15.2	21.3	2.0	7.0	
$Earning/Rank	17.6(2)	15.3(1)	15.5(2)	6.8(3)	9.2(2)	14.2(1)	12.8(1)	9.6(2)	7.4(1)	7.1(2)	1.7
Retail (%)	1.3	0.7	21.5	6.2	14.1	25.8	11.1	9.1	2.9	7.4	
$Earning/Rank	12.2(5)	9.3(5)	10.2(6)	5.2(6)	4.0(6)	4.5(7)	8.4(6)	5.1(7)	3.3(6)	4.0(5)	5.9
Producer services (%)	13.5	9.0	17.3	21.3	12.8	11.7	2.6	2.2	8.2	1.5	
$Earning/Rank	18.2(1)	11.0(4)	13.2(4)	6.1(4)	6.0(4)	11.7(2)	9.7(4)	5.5(4)	5.1(4)	3.8(6)	3.7
Consumer services (%)	0.5	4.4	9.6	2.4	5.0	0.6	7.8	6.8	58.6	4.3	
$Earning/Rank	11.2(7)	5.6(7)	9.3(7)	5.2(7)	3.6(7)	5.1(6)	7.3(7)	5.3(5)	2.7(7)	2.1(7)	6.7

Nonprofit services (%)	36.0	12.9	4.0	11.6	6.3	0.2	2.0	1.1	24.8	1.0	
$Earning/Rank	12.1(6)	7.7(6)	12.7(5)	5.5(5)	4.3(5)	7.5(5)	9.1(5)	5.3(6)	4.4(5)	4.5(4)	5.2
Public administration (%)	10.2	25.1	12.0	15.2	18.3	0.1	7.2	2.0	6.5	3.7	
$Earning/Rank	15.9(4)	13.6(3)	15.2(3)	7.5(1)	10.5(1)	7.7(4)	11.0(3)	9.8(1)	6.4(3)	7.0(3)	2.6
Services (%)	13.2	8.2	12.7	10.4	10.2	8.0	7.2	6.9	19.2	4.0	
Nonservices (%)	4.4	4.1	15.6	5.2	3.9	2.0	20.7	31.3	1.4	11.3	
All industries (%)	10.3	6.9	13.6	8.7	8.2	6.0	11.7	15.0	13.3	6.4	

[a] Agriculture-forestry-fisheries; mining and construction are not shown but are included in totals. Ranks are for average earnings among given occupations and are shown in parentheses.

Note: Underlines are for emphasis.

Source: U.S. Department of Labor, Bureau of Labor Statistics, Survey of Income and Education, 1975.

fessionals account for 36 percent of employment in the non-profit services (largely health and education) but less than 2 percent in retailing and consumer services; office clericals make up 21 percent of employment in producers services, but less than 3 percent of employment in consumer services. Managerial jobs are relatively important in distributive services, retailing, and producers services, and much less important in the remaining services.

Although these differences in occupational structure influence overall earnings in the industry categories, differences in earnings levels among industries reflect other factors as well. Some industries pay relatively well across occupations, others relatively poorly. This is readily seen in Table 4.1, where average earnings in each occupation are ranked separately *among* industries. When these ranks of the various occupations are compared *within* given industries, they are found to vary little in most instances. Occupations in the distributive services show an average rank of 1.7, with all occupations ranking first or second except office clericals, which rank third. Occupations in manufacturing have the second-highest average ranking, 2.2, followed by occupations in public administration, 2.6, and in producer services, 3.7. The lowest rankings are in nonprofit, 5.2, retail, 5.9, and consumer services, 6.7. Interestingly, occupations within producer services show the greatest discrepancy among ranks: professionals rank first in earnings and sales persons second, but seven of the eight remaining occupations rank fourth, and laborers, a relatively unimportant category, rank sixth.

Just how the combined effects of overall industry earnings tendencies and occupational distribution works out in terms of the earnings distribution of each of the industry groups is summarized in Table 4.2, which shows for each industry the percentage of employment falling within each of five income classes (rough quintiles of total employment arrayed by annual earnings).[2] The earnings profiles of the various industry groups vary sharply. Consumer services and retailing are essentially low-pay industries, not only because earnings are relatively low across occupations but because these service groups are heavily weighted with low-earnings occupations. Distributive services and public administration, on the other hand, are characterized by few poorly paid jobs, while for producers services and nonprofit services, the distribution shows concentrations of employment in both well- and poorly-paid employment. For services as a whole, the important observation is that there tend to be heavy concentration of employment in better-than-average and in poorer-than-average jobs. In contrast, in manufacturing and construction the distributions are more heavily weighted toward medium and above-average income jobs.

Of course, there are variations in employment conditions among the individual industries that account for some of these deficiencies. For example, the differences in earnings between the health and the educational services within the nonprofit services (Table 4.2) are due in considerable measure to the part-year nature of employment of professionals and others in the educational system. Nevertheless, the indus-

Table 4.2 Percentage Distribution of Employment among Earnings Classes (Quintiles) for Industry Groups and U.S. Economy, 1975

	Earnings quintiles				
	Top	2nd	3rd	4th	Lowest
Industry groups[a]	($12,000 and over)	($9,500– 11,999)	($7,000– 9,499)	($4,500– 6,999)	(Below $4,500)
Manufacturing	26.2	20.0	35.7	16.4	1.7
Construction	18.0	2.0	60.9	18.8	.4
Distributive services	44.2	16.7	29.2	9.4	.4
Retail	1.2	22.0	16.7	16.4	43.7
Producer services	30.8	22.2	1.3	44.3	1.5
Consumer services	.2	3.9	13.2	13.4	69.3
Nonprofit services	6.8	34.1	10.7	32.6	15.8
Health	17.3	2.2	24.2	56.2	.1
Education	—	54.6	2.1	17.4	26.0
Public administration	47.1	27.4	15.2	10.1	—
Total employment	18.9	19.6	23.0	20.0	18.5

[a] Agriculture, fisheries and mining not shown.

Note: Largest two quintiles underlined for emphasis. Earnings classes were determined by arraying all industry-occupation cells according to average earnings in individual cells and dividing the range of earnings by rough quintiles of employment in the array.

Source: U.S. Department of Labor, Bureau of Labor Statistics, *Survey of Income and Education*, 1975.

trial groupings may be regarded as appropriate for showing the major compositional tendencies.

The foregoing analysis tells us much about the significance of growing service employment in the economy. The shift to services has been a shift to activities with occupational and earnings characteristics that differ sharply from those obtaining in a majority of goods-producing activities. But the service groupings differ sharply among themselves. Accordingly, the pattern of future changes in earnings will be determined by which types of services demonstrate the fastest rates of employment growth and by how much the mix of occupations and the relative earnings levels within these occupations change in the years ahead.

The analysis of employment changes that follows highlights recent changes in service employment and examines evidences of shifts in the importance of occupations within service groups in order to shed light on the directions in which current trends within the economy may be carrying us.

Changes in Occupations. This analysis focuses on two periods that are generally representative of the sixties and seventies, 1960– 1967 and 1970– 1976.[3] They are periods that differed sharply. The years 1960– 1967 were characterized by rapid growth of total employment, during which there was a substantial increase in manufacturing employment and rapid expansion of health and educational services and of public administration. Producer services also grew at rates substantially above the national level, although distributive services, retailing, and consumer services grew more slowly.

In contrast, the seventies were years of substantially diminished growth, during which employment in the manufacturing sector declined. Again, growth rates among the services differed significantly. The distributive services grew at the national rate, and public administration employment at a rate only slightly higher. Trends within the nonprofit services differed as educational services slowed down under the impact of a stabilizing youth cohort, while health services continued to grow rapidly. Producer services continued to grow rapidly, and retail employment expanded at a rate higher than that of the economy as a whole.

These divergent trends reflect not only changing demand

but the effect of a variety of supply side forces, including differential impacts of technology and applications of human and physical capital upon various activities within the system. It is not our purpose to analyze these forces and the way they have impacted the services, but rather to examine the extent of changes that have occurred and to make rough estimates of the effect these changes have had on the composition of earnings.

It is of critical importance to determine whether given occupations have grown or failed to grow in step with total employment in specific service and nonservice industries. This is most readily measured by computing the hypothetical growth (decline) of each occupation in each industry (assuming that occupation and sex composition remain unchanged during a given period) and comparing this change with the actual change that occurred. The difference is designated as "shift" and indicates the amount by which actual change in employment in a given occupation was greater (or less) than would have been expected in light of industry growth. Aggregate measures of hypothetical change, actual change, and shift in each occupation are shown separately for services and nonservices in Appendix Table A.1.

The breakdown of this occupational shift is summarized in Table 4.3. Here we find hints of new trends that are at work but that may be obscured by abnormally high or low rates of change in individual industry employment. Shift, which may be either positive or negative, measures the extent to which an occupation grows faster than its industry, fails to grow as fast as its industry (even though the occupation may grow very fast indeed), or fails to decline as fast as its industry. Such changes may (but need not) be harbingers of new trends in the years ahead.

Although the shift estimates represent only rough statements of tendencies toward growth or decline and deserve the most detailed analysis and evaluation before conclusive statements can be made, several developments can be noted with some confidence.

The clearest pertains to the nonservices, largely manufacturing. In manufacturing, the seventies brought a significant departure from earlier trends. During the sixties a marked

Table 4.3 Analysis of Occupational "Shift" in Selected Industries, 1960 to 1967 and 1970 to 1976

Occupation	Total nonservices[b]	Mfg.	Total services	Distributive services	Retail	Producer services	Mainly consumer services	Nonprofit services	Public administration
					1960—1967				
"Shift"[a]									
Total	0	0	0	0	0	0	0	0	0
Professional	112,772	97,621	401,441	34,668	1,873	-21,764	29,592	286,255	70,817
Technical	29,313	23,355	74,176	45,992	2,290	-2,760	16,261	-8,433	20,826
Manager	-143,063	-20,035	-354,759	-37,719	-310,947	9,816	-1,078	-8,273	-6,558
Office clerical	42,415	28,867	86,354	18,757	34,033	-21,915	24,640	-149,815	7,946
Nonoffice clerical	4,258	-6,259	171,816	-6,273	203,302	51,316	82,396	-78,695	-80,230
Sales workers	-37,388	-37,362	-137,059	-25,580	-73,269	-41,058	7,396	-4,144	-404
Craft workers	-510	-41,775	159,925	-33,954	87,953	13,392	50,948	-29,309	2,987
Operatives	379,860	305,153	68,527	-3,823	43,876	35,146	17,531	-21,057	-3,146
Service workers	-74,419	-73,105	-242,453	-15,612	-14,520	-27,222	-191,620	24,383	-17,862
Laborers	-313,238	-294,460	-55,260	-44,364	25,409	5,049	-36,066	-10,912	5,624

"Shift"ᵃ

	1970–1976								
Total	0	0	0	0	0	0	0	0	0
Professional	82,958	71,000	-311,234	28,995	4,916	-19,277	13,979	-421,469	82,628
Technical	111,360	92,233	504,245	33,934	13,941	97,576	87,186	160,572	111,135
Manager	97,699	155,214	483,923	95,452	195,197	68,185	29,873	101,044	-5,828
Office clerical	-22,016	-36,774	-87,320	-58,841	7,417	-158,006	35,199	117,351	-30,440
Nonoffice clerical	-47,116	-60,157	30,868	-99,208	92,376	-40,482	80,836	153,736	-156,390
Sales	15,268	6,481	126,106	44,778	-261,962	73,794	14,616	3,436	-768
Craft workers	73,593	40,887	153,546	-7,297	20,478	-13,802	145,594	27,156	-18,583
Operatives	-118,849	-139,267	-75,433	28,627	-109,222	-8,342	-39,236	41,509	11,231
Service workers	-65,087	-60,408	-631,501	-19,782	-22,738	-475	-381,271	-207,352	117
Laborers	-127,810	-69,209	59,012	-46,558	59,603	829	14,224	24,016	6,898

ᵃSee text for definition of "shift."
ᵇIncludes agriculture, mining, and construction (not shown) as well as manufacturing.

Source: U.S. Department of Labor, Bureau of Labor Statistics, *Tomorrow's Manpower Needs, Industry-Occupational Matrix*, Microdata, 1960, 1967, 1970, 1976.

expansion in plant activities (operatives) was accompanied by heavy increases in office clericals and professionals, with some shift toward increased use of technicians. The seventies brought a sharp cutback of operatives and clericals, both office and nonoffice, but a continued buildup of professionals and technicians, this time with reduced attention to expanding professional staffs and increased emphasis on the hiring of technicians. Even more important, the seventies brought a rapid increase in managerial and supervisory personnel.

All this is consistent with our previous discussion of the service transformation within manufacturing — the movement toward greater emphasis on functions at the central administrative office level, with greater use of managerial, professional, and technical staff. It also suggests the beginning of a trend away from the use of clerical personnel, reflecting, at least in part, the increased application of computer technology.

The case of public administration is largely one of upgrading. During the sixties and seventies, there were shifts toward professional and technical personnel — more toward technicians and somewhat less toward professionals in the most recent period. Shifts away from nonoffice clericals in the sixties were extended to both office and nonoffice clericals during the seventies.

The tendency toward a positive shift in professionals is noted for most industrial groupings. The exceptions during the seventies are found only in nonprofit services (a substantial negative shift, probably associated with efforts to adjust to a declining student level in the educational services) and in both the sixties and seventies in producer services, where the small unfavorable shift appears to be of little significance. (There was roughly a quarter of a million net increase in professionals as producer services grew rapidly during the seventies; see Appendix Table A.1.)

For technicians, significant positive employment shift characterized all industrial groups in the seventies and most groups during the sixties. Comparison of the trends in professionals and technicians suggests that the growth trend for technicians is strengthening; the trend for professionals may be weakening somewhat.

The picture for clericals is less clear, for experience differs among industries. A trend toward some lessening of importance of both office and nonoffice clericals is found in the seventies for producer and distributive services as well as for manufacturing and public administration, as was observed above. In retailing, consumer services, and the nonprofit services, however, shift indicates continuation of the strong positive trend.

The managerial classification is difficult to analyze since it includes both managers of small establishments (whether branches, franchises, or independent) and executive personnel of large firms. The negative shift in managers during the sixties occurred principally in retailing, but some negative shift is noted in all the industrial groups shown, except producer services.

During the seventies, however, all service industries except public administration show positive shift in managers. In producers and distributive services this is most likely explainable in terms of the buildup of administrative staffs in larger firms in areas such as accounting, advertising, airlines, trucking, banking, investment, and insurance. In nonprofit services it is probably again explained chiefly in terms of increase in administrative overhead. In consumer services and in retailing, however, the more probable explanation would seem to be a rising importance of small establishments — branches, franchised outlets, and independents. The matter deserves careful investigation.

Finally, the substantial negative shift in the occupational classification "service workers" presents something of a puzzle. In both periods the major share is accounted for by the very sharp decline in domestic servants, classified within the consumer services. Yet some negative shift is observed in virtually all industry groups during both the sixties and seventies. One possible explanation is that illegal immigrants were increasingly hired for these menial tasks, and such workers are not recorded in the employment surveys. Another is that service workers tend to be upgraded in their titles (e.g., from service workers to operatives) as well as in the trappings of their work (uniforms, etc.) in an effort to improve morale and increase efficiency. A third is that through improved organization and increased reliance on technology, significant headway is being made toward economizing on this traditionally relatively low productive labor.

Changes in Earnings Structure. When average 1975 earnings for each occupational-industrial cell are applied to employment changes, rough estimates of the effect of employment changes in distribution of earnings can be made for the two periods 1960– 1967 and 1970– 1976. We observe that in both periods, changes in service employment acted to reinforce the earnings distribution already observed previously for services during the year 1975: larger shares of employment in the higher and lower earnings categories, a smaller share in the middle category. Moreover, the tendency toward divergence was somewhat stronger in services during the seventies than during the sixties, as shown in Table 4.4.

It may be asked why, given the tendency toward a modification of growth trends in clerical and service workers, as measured in terms of shift, there were disproportionate increases in low-paying service jobs. The answer appears to lie in the continued vigorous growth in health services and the more rapid growth of retailing and consumer services (largely res-

Table 4.4 Percentage Distribution of Job Increases and Job Decreases among Earnings Classes. All Services, 1960–1967 and 1970–1976

Earnings Class[a]	Increases		Decreases	
	1960–67	1970–76	1960–67	1970–76
$12,000 and more	16.0	18.8	7.9	4.5
$ 9,500–11,999	23.9	20.6	43.2	8.7
$ 7,000– 9,499	11.6	12.4	23.3	13.6
$ 4,500– 6,999	28.1	25.4	2.4	12.4
Less than $4,500	20.4	22.8	23.1	60.8
Total	100.0	100.0	100.0	100.0
Number of increases (decreases) in thousands	7,913.8	9,274.4	(426.9)	(615.7)

[a] Job increases (decreases) computed for each industry–occupation cell and assigned to earnings class on basis of 1975 earnings in that cell.

Source: U.S. Department of Labor, Bureau of Labor Statistics, *Tomorrow's Manpower Needs, Industry-Occupational Matrix,* Microdata 1960, 1967, 1970, and 1976, and *Survey of Income and Education,* 1975.

taurants), both heavy employers of low-income workers during the second period.

In nonservices (not shown here), there was a tendency for growth to focus on the upper half of the distribution and for attrition to occur disproportionately in the middle income range. This was particularly true during the seventies when there were heavy job decreases in the manufacturing sector.

For the U.S. economy, the net result of combined job increases and decreases in services and nonservices has been a tendency in both periods for employment growth to be greater in the upper and lower earnings ranges than in the middle. This tendency appears to have strengthened somewhat in the most recent period (see Table 4.5).

These data are, of course, only estimates based on assumptions of a constancy of relative incomes (at 1975 levels) in each industry-occupational subgroup. They may differ to the extent that relative wages or the internal composition of individual subgroups are changing. Yet the patterns observed are roughly consistent over two decades and strongly suggest that significant changes in earnings distribution are at work.

Such a finding raises serious questions about what is taking place in the U.S. economy. Who are the workers engaged in

Table 4.5 Percentage Distribution of Job Increases and Job Decreases among Earnings Classes. All Industries, 1960–1967 and 1970–1976

Earnings Class[a]	Increases		Decreases	
	1960–67	1970–76	1960–67	1970–76
$12,000 and more	18.1	21.9	3.2	7.9
$ 9,500–11,000	22.7	19.4	11.4	11.2
$ 7,000– 9,499	21.3	14.3	74.6	35.7
$ 4,500– 6,900	23.1	23.0	6.0	22.8
Less than $4,500	14.8	21.4	4.8	22.3
Total	100.0	100.0	100.0	100.0
Number increases (decreases) in thousands	10,982.0	10,541.8	(2,388.0)	(1,701.4)

[a] Job increaes (decreases) computed for each industry-occupation cell and assigned to earnings class on basis of 1975 earnings in that cell.
Source: Same as Table 4.4.

lower wage and salary occupations? What factors are working to create jobs disproportionately in the upper and lower ranges of the scale? To what extent are opportunities to move up the income ladder improving or declining? To what extent do jobs with low income offer oversetting advantages of flexibility in hours and security of tenure?

These are questions that deserve detailed investigation beyond the scope of this monograph. Some additional light can be shed, however, by examining briefly some important characteristics of employment in the services, including the role of women, part-time employment, some selected attributes related to "sheltering," and the level of educational attainment.

Women's Role in the Service Workforce

That employment of women has risen rapidly in the postwar years is now widely recognized. Between 1950 and 1976, 60 percent of the total increase in the size of the labor force was accounted for by women, even though women were outnumbered by men by nearly 2.5 to 1 in 1950 (Ginzberg 1977). Moreover, the increase in female employment has been closely identified with the growth of services. During the decade of the sixties, 81 percent of the total increase in female employment was accounted for by the services. In 1975 (the latest year for which industry-occupation breakdowns are available), 49 percent of service jobs were held by women, and 24 percent of nonservice jobs.

If women are playing such an important role in services, at least in terms of numbers, what kind of jobs do they hold? The evidence seems clear that female employment is largely confined to a restricted number of relatively poorly paid occupational categories. In only 26 of the 60 service industry-occupation subgroups (six industry, ten occupation groups cross-classified) was the percentage of female employment higher than 41 percent (women's share of total national employment); and all but one of these 26 occupational industry subgroups were in occupational classes with relatively low average earnings: office clericals, nonoffice clericals, operatives, service workers, and laborers. The generally low earnings that characterize those industry-occupational subgroups with relatively high female employment is readily observed in Table 4.6.

There is evidence of some upgrading of employment for women, however (Stanback 1979): during the period 1970–1977 the most striking change occurred in the managerial occupational category, where growth of female employment occurred at a rate of more than 10 percent per annum and accounted for 12 percent of employment gains by women.[4] Another broad occupational classification that was a source of improvement was "professionals, technicians, and kindred" (PTK), which provided almost a fifth of all female job increases. These were not necessarily top-level jobs, but no doubt represented better than average career opportunities for women.

On the other hand, 31 percent of female job increases were accounted for by clerical workers, 28 percent by service workers, and 11 percent by craft workers, sales workers, and laborers. As we have seen, these occupations for the most part pay relatively low wages.

Other Characteristics of Service Employment

In her *Labor Markets: Segments and Shelters,* Marcia Freedman (1976) examined a variety of structural and demographic characteristics to determine the extent to which variations in each accounted for variations in average earnings in detailed occupation-industry subgroups of the U.S. workforce in the

---

Table 4.6 Number of Service Industry-Occupational Subgroups with Higher than Average Female Employment by Earnings Classes, 1975

Earnings class	Number of subgroups with higher than average female employment
$12,000 and more	0
$ 9,500–11,999	0
$ 7,000– 9,499	3
$ 4,500– 6,999	14
Less than $4,500	9
Total	26

Note: There are 60 service industry-occupational subgroups (six industries, ten occupations cross-classified).
Source: Same as Table 4.4.

year 1970.[5] All exerted a significant influence on earnings levels, and all must be regarded as important in considering the nature of work in the services.

Part-Time Employment. By far the greatest variance in earnings within the workforce was accounted for by the percentage of workers employed full time, full year. Less than full-time work places a major constraint on earnings. Although such work is desirable for many, for others it is acceptable only because better job opportunities are not available.

The percentage of workers employed full time, full year in 1975 was significantly lower, 57 percent, in services than in nonservice, 62 percent. There was, however, considerable variation among service industries, as shown in Table 4.7.

Table 4.7   **Percentage of Employment Full Time/Full Year in Service Industries, 1975**

Service industries	Percentage of employment, full time/full year
Distributive services	73.8
Public administration	80.9
Producer services	67.2
Mainly consumer	34.2
Retail	51.3
Nonprofit services	54.2

Source: Same as Table 4.4.

Table 4.8   **Number of Service Industry-Occupational Subgroups with Lower than Average Full-Time/Full-Year Employment by Earnings Classes, 1975**

Earnings class	Number of industry-occupation subgroups with % of full-time, full-year employment below U.S. average
$12,000 and more	0
$ 9,500–11,999	0
$ 7,000– 9,499	4
$ 4,500– 6,999	14
Less than $4,500	9
Total	27

Note: There are 60 service industry-occupational subgroups (six industries, ten occupations cross-classified).
Source: Same as Table 4.4.

Moreover, relatively low percentages of full-time, full-year employment in service occupation-industry subgroups were strongly associated with relatively low average annual earnings, as shown in Table 4.8.

Sheltering. Employment varies widely in terms of the extent to which the worker finds security in job tenure, opportunities for fringe benefits, availability of grievance procedures, and opportunities for advancement to more responsible and better paid work. Such job characteristics may be strongly influenced by certain structural attributes, which include size of establishment, class of worker, internal labor market characteristics, licensing, accreditation, and collective bargaining. These were analyzed in some detail for the entire workforce by Freedman (1976), and briefly for services by Stanback (1979).

It is important to understand to what extent structural attributes may influence characteristics of the job itself. *Firm size* is important in that large firms have traditionally tended to make use of management procedures and labor-management arrangements that contribute to greater job security (e.g., codified work rules, grievance procedures, protection against arbitrary personnel decisions, seniority practices, and maintenance of employment in the face of technological changes). In general, larger firms have tended to offer greater security, greater equity in terms of working arrangements, and greater opportunities for advancement than small firms. At the same time, there are indications that these characteristics of employment in large firms may be changing with the emergence of new occupations and the decline of traditional ones. The result may be a decrease in opportunity for upward mobility (Stanback and Noyelle, 1981).

Class of worker (identified in terms of whether the job is classified as private wage and salary, government, or self-employed) has varying significance in the labor marketplace. Government employment provides higher annual earnings and more stable employment for most, but not all, occupations. Private wage and salary employment is often associated with responsible jobs in large organizations, yet there are many low-income workers who are employed on a private wage or salary basis. Similarly, self-employed workers may vary widely in terms of earnings, depending on training and accreditation among professionals, experience and entrepreneurial skills among owner-managers, and skill, knowledge, and training among sales and craft workers.

The term *internal labor market* relates to the extent that firms comprise labor markets within themselves, offering opportunities for promotion, upgrading, and shifts to more desirable types of work. Such "internal" markets are likely to be found only in large firms or government and need not exist for all occupations within such organizations.

Finally, bargaining factors — *licensing-accreditation* and *union membership* — may be of considerable importance. Licensing and accreditation strengthen occupational distinctions and may provide a basis for restricting entry into a given type of professional or technical employment. There has been a strong trend in recent years toward increased licensing and formal accreditation in a number of areas, especially among technicians in the health delivery services.

Unions are most important for worker protection where licensing and accreditation are not possible. Historically, union organization has been most widespread among crafts and in certain large and well-established industries, industries typically dominated by a handful of major firms. Unionization has increased significantly among service and maintenance personnel in health and educational institutions and among public school teachers since the 1960s, but has not grown as rapidly as white collar employment except among public employees,where it has made large gains.

Analysis of the extent of sheltering in the services in 1970 reveals a wide variation in employment structural characteristics among the industry-occupation subgroups.[6] Only in certain segments of the services (those with medium and high average earnings) is there evidence of significant sheltering for an important share of workers. The high-income subgroups that were so characterized were principally professionals in producers services and health services (from licensing accreditation), managers in wholesaling and FIRE (from internal labor markets), and professionals and technicians in public administration (from very large establishment size and internal labor markets). Medium-income workers who appeared to enjoy significant sheltering were principally professionals in education (from licensing accreditation and large establishment size), managers and clericals in public administration (from large establishment size), and sales workers in durable retailing (from very large establishment size, internal labor market, and collective bargaining).

There were also a restricted number of subgroups in which earnings were above average, but there was little evidence of sheltering. For these subgroups (largely managers and wholesale sales persons), higher than average earnings may be regarded largely as a reflection of levels of responsibility or skills demanded of the workers.

When the lower-income subgroups are examined there is little evidence of shelter. Work is largely on a private wage and salary basis, but establishment size is typically medium or small. Internal labor market structure and collective bargaining are of little importance. For this broad group of workers in services, work is part time, poorly paid, and characterized by little promise of advancement.

Educational Characteristics. In an earlier study Fuchs (1968) found that there was a higher level of educational attainment in the services than in goods. This is confirmed by data presented in Table 4.9. While only selected services are shown, it is clear that for most activities educational attainment is higher in the services than in manufacturing, although for some, such as personal services and services to dwellings and other buildings, it is roughly the same or lower. The principal conclusion is, once again, that there is a very large discrepancy between the quality and earnings level of upper and lower level services employment.

Young Workers and Minorities. It is unfortunate that this must be written a decade after the last census, for demographic characteristics have changed significantly in the intervening years. In 1970, the analysis of employment by income and age showed that the percentage of young workers in low income jobs was significantly higher in services than in nonservices.[7] This accords with general observation: jobs in retailing and consumer services have become the major entry points into the labor market in postwar America, in contrast to an earlier day when young people began work on the farm or in the

Table 4.9 Percentage Distribution of Employment by Number of Years of Education: Manufacturing, All Services, and Selected Service Classifications, 1970

| | Years of high school | | Years of college | | Years of post-graduate work |
| | | | Community college | | |
	0–8	9–12	13–14	15–16	17–18
Manufacturing	28.8	57.7	3.0	6.0	4.0
All services[a]	15.1	45.6	10.5	15.3	13.6
Personal services[b]	28.0	54.9	6.8	7.2	2.3
Business services[c]	18.8	56.5	10.0	8.8	5.9
Services to dwelling and other buildings	(30.7)	(57.2)	(6.9)	(3.7)	(1.5)
Detective	(28.9)	(57.6)	(7.4)	(4.2)	
Business service not elsewhere classified	(13.4)	(59.2)	(12.1)	(9.6)	(5.5)
Temporary help supply	(10.3)	(50.8)	(12.5)	(14.6)	(11.8)
Advertising	(9.9)	(52.1)	(13.2)	(14.8)	(10.0)
Research and development laboratories	(8.4)	(39.8)	(12.0)	(20.7)	(19.3)
Computer programming and other software services	(8.3)	(47.6)	(12.8)	(17.0)	(14.2)
Management consulting and public relations	(7.1)	(45.0)	(13.1)	(18.8)	(16.0)

[a]Includes all 2-digit SIC service classifications. Note only two 2-digit service classifications (personal services and business services) are shown below.
[b]SIC Number 72.
[c]SIC Number 73 (misc. business services). Classifications listed below are subclassifications.
Note: Based on a 5% sample of the population 25 years and older. The table is derived by way of matrix multiplication of industry by occupation and educational attainment by occupation matrices.
Source: U.S. Census Bureau, 1970 Census of Population, Subject Reports, PC(2)-7C: *Occupation by Industry*; PC(2)-5B: *Educational Attainment.*

factory. Today, jobs in manufacturing are likely to pay the young worker more and to be more difficult to acquire.

Similarly, in 1970, a disproportionately large share of employment of nonwhites in services was characterized by low incomes as compared to jobs for nonwhites in nonservices. It is likely that the same is true today, although we do know that for some minority groups, especially married black males over 25 years of age, there has been a very sharp improvement.

Summary and Implications

The preceding analysis makes it possible to draw a rough profile of service employment and to observe certain patterns of change. We have seen that jobs in the service industries and occupations vary widely in earnings but tend to fall into a rough dichotomy: good jobs and bad jobs. Growth trends appear to be reenforcing this tendency at least to a modest extent. Behind these earnings characteristics lie basic differences between work characteristics. Poorly paid service jobs are likely to be poorly sheltered and to be part time in nature. They are also more likely to be held by women, young people, or members of minority groups than are better paid service jobs or nonservice jobs in general.

When we begin to probe into the possible new directions in which growth in the services is carrying us, there are but a few straws in the wind. The negative tendencies in the shift measures for the service worker and clerical occupational groups suggest incipient movements away from low income service employment, while the robust growth in technicians is in accord with the widely held view that growth of the services is upgrading employment in the U.S. economy.

Nevertheless, there remain persuasive reasons to expect that the trends of the past two decades toward parallel growth of good and bad jobs will not be altered sharply in the years ahead. On one hand, there continues to be substantial growth among small businesses, especially in retailing and consumer services. On the other, there is abundant evidence that a very large support system of relatively low skill clerical and service-worker type jobs is still required in order for the more elite and well-paid sectors of professionals, managers, and technicians to carry out their daily tasks under existing institutional and organizational arrangements.

Finally, there remains the question about which there is so much concern: How rapidly will women be able to make advances in a job market in which services appear to continue to increase in importance? Perhaps the fundamental observation is that the services are, indeed, more soft handed, more suitable to utilizing the abilities of women than were the old industrial jobs. This is not likely to change, and women, perhaps gradually, but nevertheless inevitably, will be substantial beneficiaries.

Notes

[1]The occupational classification "service worker" must be distinguished from the generic term, which simply refers to those employed in the services. The occupational classification includes, for example, cooks and housekeepers, cleaning workers, food service workers, and health service workers.

[2]Average earnings in each industry occupation cell (subgroup) were arrayed from highest to lowest for the workforce with employment indicated for each cell. Roughly the top fifth of employment measured in terms of earning were identified as the top quintile, the next fifth as the second quintile, etc. The quintile groupings were not broken at exact fifths of the workforce where there were clusters of employment around cutoff points. Rather, the earnings limits of each "quintile" were adjusted to avoid such clusters. Nevertheless, the groupings do approximate rough fifths of the workforce. The range of earnings for each quintile includes the earnings within the portion of the array defined by that quintile.

[3]Freedman (1980) states, "The choice of the 1960-67 period is a deliberate attempt to differentiate from those of the seventies. A critical divergence in trends occurred toward the end of the sixties, a divergence that the 1960-70 comparisons obscure, but which emerges clearly in the 1970-76 data" (p. 11, chapter 5).

[4]The data for these most recent years were available only on an occupational basis. They were not cross-classified by industry.

[5]The characteristics related to percentage with full-time, full-year employment, class of worker, internal labor market, establishment size, licensing and accreditation, and collective bargaining. She has replicated this analysis for 1976 with similar results (Freedman 1980).

[6]The findings reported here are drawn directly from Stanback (1979), pp. 51 – 52.

[7]Based on ibid., pp. 49– 57.

5. The Changing Urban Landscape and the Location of Economic Activities

To discuss the transformation of the economic system in spatial terms brings to the fore a whole range of issues which otherwise tends to be subordinated: issues of agglomeration economies, scale economies, and the importance of market size for the entry and survival of firms.

Spatial analysis makes clear the importance of a careful analytical breakdown of the services. Because spatial development in recent decades has tended to foster metropolitan specialization and unevenness of development of the economic landscape, many of the trends exhibited by the services have tended to be sharpened and accentuated at the level of individual places. This is helpful for the researcher, who must often struggle with the identification of important underlying structural tendencies diluted by many less important ones.

A discussion of the changing urban landscape should open with two important observations. First, the continuing urbanization of our population, although often taken for granted, deserves some careful thought. There is nothing inevitable or uncontrollable about it. Rather it is a reflection of very powerful socio-economic forces at work among consumers, producers, and even government. Second, cities are very much artifacts of society, in that they tend to be manipulated and transformed to adjust to the requirements of new modes of public and private life or new forms of work. For example, the suburban explosion after the war responded to a demand for

a certain type of individual lifestyle popular at the time, in
much the same way that recent tendencies toward "gentrification" or "rural renaissance" express the demands of younger
generations.[1] Likewise, skyscrapers and office buildings have
replaced the factories of a former era to fulfill the requirements of the dominant form of work at hand. Thus, the
unending transformation of the physical landscape both mir-
rors and contributes to the structural changes at work in the
economy.

The shift toward services has been accompanied by a rise of
service employment in the economies of individual places and
by a restructuring of the urban hierarchy.[2] In part the growth
of services has been more or less ubiquitous. The more basic
consumer, retailing, and local government services are essentially residentiary and must be provided in relative proximity
to people everywhere. Other services, however, must be concentrated, to a greater or lesser extent, because of the need to
attain necessary economies of scale, to be near each other
(agglomeration economies), and to be close to large metropolitan markets. These latter services are led by the producer services, certain strategic distributive services (especially airports), the producer-service-like functions provided
by major corporate headquarters, and some key government
and educational services. They have become the primary
wealth- and development-producing activities in the economic base of numerous cities. In short, they have, like manufacturing in an earlier day, spear-headed the economic
transformation of many metropolitan places in recent times
(Duncan and Lieberson 1970, Stanback and Knight 1970).

In the paragraphs that follow, we review some of the issues
involved in this transformation of the urban system by raising
some basic questions: Where have services grown the fastest?
Where have the manufacturing jobs gone? How deeply has
the overall urban system been transformed? Which places
have fared the best, which the worst?

Two Concepts: Export Specialization of Metropolitan Places and Urban Hierarchy

A basic concept that underlies most urban economic analysis is
that of export specialization of metropolitan places.[3] Urban

economists find it useful to conceive of metropolitan places as relatively closed economies trading with one another and thus engaged in both export and residentiary activities. Residentiary activities are, simply, those that provide for the needs of those who live and work in the immediate area and that depend directly on the purchasing power of residents. Export activities provide for the needs of users outside the area and are the principal source of income with which local residents may import goods and services from other places.

Without denying the importance and the export nature of distributive (especially wholesaling) and producer (especially financing) services in key cities of the urban hierarchy in earlier times, it is safe to argue that for decades (since the advent of industrialization) manufacturing constituted the major export industry of most cities. With the dispersal of production plants to outlying or distant areas and the rising importance of services, however, it is increasingly headquarters, producers services, distributive services, nonprofit services, and public sector services that constitute the export base of large places.

The concept of urban hierarchy is based on the recognition that there exists a logical arrangement among cities, in terms of the level of their economic specialization, in which population size is an important correlate. The urban system is regarded as made up of a few very large centers, which are the most diversified and the best equipped to provide for extremely specialized goods and services to be exported elsewhere in the system, a somewhat larger number of medium size cities characterized by their slightly lesser diversification and specialization, a much larger number of relatively small places engaged in activities characterized by significantly less diversification and specialization, and so forth. At the same time, however, as Dunn (1980) and Pred (1977) have argued and as the following presentation confirms, the strict relationship between specialization and diversification of economic base, on the one hand, and population size, on the other, is insufficient to explain the structure of the urban system in an economy in which cities are becoming increasingly interdependent.

At the heart of these new developments is the tendency for

the large corporation to restrict each step of the processes of product development, production, distribution, financing, or sales promotion, to increasingly specialized centers. Input-output relationships tend to be articulated increasingly more on a systemwide basis. This means that import substitution is less likely to take place as a given metropolitan area grows than was true of an earlier era. Thus increasingly we find, side by side, cities that provide for wide ranges of services and functions and cities of comparable size that thrive on a very selective set of activities. This is a very fundamental dimension of the urban transformation at work.

Recent Locational Tendencies of Manufacturing and Service Employment

For purposes of analysis, the system of cities is segmented into five populaton size layers (Table 5.1).

Table 5.2 shows the average distribution of sectoral employment by size group of metropolitan places and the resulting employment location quotient of each sector for 1959 and 1976. For ease in reading the results, location quotients have been multiplied by 100.[4] For simplicity in computation and presentation, data on the Size 5 SMSAs have been combined with those of nonmetropolitan and rural counties.

Locational tendencies revealed by Table 5.2 fall under three general patterns largely defined in terms of three broad

Table 5.1   Number of Standard Metropolitan Statistical Areas (SMSAs) by Population Size Groups, 1976

Size group of SMSAs	1976 population range of SMSAs[a]	1976 number of SMSAs
Size 1	more than 2 million	17
Size 2	1 to 2 million	19
Size 3	0.5 to 1 million	39
Size 4	0.25 to 0.5 million	65
Size 5	Less than 0.25 million	126
Total		266

[a]*Standard Metropolitan Statistical Areas* are defined in terms of aggregates of counties by the Bureau of the Census.
Source: U.S. Department of Commerce, Bureau of the Census, *Current Population Reports*, series P-25.

groups of industries: first, the *mostly residentiary services* (retail, consumer services, and part of nonprofit services and government); second, *mostly export services* (complex of corporate activities,[5] distributive services, and part of nonprofit services and government); third, *the manufacturing sector.*

The Residentiary Services. The shares of employment accounted for by residentiary services vary least across the size hierarchy of cities. This is not a surprising finding, but simply says something which has long been known by urban economists: the single most important economic factor that determines the location of retail and other consumer services is the *proximity to consumers.* Accordingly, the share of employment (and thus the location quotient) is likely to be roughly the same in all places. This is true also of local government, local hospitals, or local teaching institutions. The size of such service delivery establishments tends to be small, reflecting the very limits imposed by the market area they serve. This does not entirely rule out the possibility of *economies of scale,* however. Large department stores, for example, can operate more efficiently than smaller ones do, assuming that a certain population threshold is there to ensure their existence.

The Export Services. The behavior of the second group of services is best exemplified by the complex of corporate activities and the distributive services. The general rule here is that the larger the place, the higher the concentration in these export services — the greatest variation being demonstrated by the complex of corporate activities in which the largest places have held an unequivocal advantage. The period between 1959 and 1976 did demonstrate a slight shift in the location of these services, however, from Size 1 SMSAs toward Size 2 and Size 3 SMSAs, while Size 4 and Size 5 places lost even further ground. This shift is fairly important and deserves an analysis in and of itself, to which we return in a later section.

Thus we see that *size* and *agglomeration economies* have been major determinants of the location of export services. As the need for developmental and administrative functions of the large manufacturing or service corporations has increased, these institutions have chosen to expand their head offices and related installations in major urban centers in proximity to producer-service firms rather than near their plants or

Table 5.2 Distribution of Employment by Major Industry Groupings and by Size Group of SMSAs, 1959 and 1976

	Size 1				Size 2			
	LQ 1959	LQ 1976	E. share 1959	E. share 1976	LQ 1959	LQ 1976	E. share 1959	E. share 1976
Manufacturing	99.0	90.5	31.1	20.7	108.3	89.6	34.0	20.5
Distributive services	112.6	112.6	13.3	11.7	114.4	112.6	13.5	11.7
Complex of corporate activities	141.6	136.4	14.4	20.0	110.3	112.7	11.2	16.6
Retail	91.5	90.9	13.9	14.5	98.3	106.1	14.9	17.0
Mainly consumer services	104.4	100.0	4.7	4.3	117.8	116.3	5.3	5.0
Nonprofit	105.7	109.2	3.7	7.1	100.0	100.0	3.5	6.5
Government	84.0	86.8	13.8 ·	16.9	77.8	89.3	12.7	17.4
All industries			100.0	100.0			100.0	100.0

Note: LQ = location quotient; E. share = employment share. "Others" include size 5 SMSAs and all remaining urban and rural counties of the nation.
Source: *County Business Patterns,* 1959 and 1976. From T. Noyelle, and T. Stanback *Economic Transformation in American Cities*, (forthcoming) 1981.

Table 5.2 (continued)

Size 3				Size 4				Others				Total U.S.	
LQ 1959	LQ 1976	E. share 1959	E. share 1976	LQ 1959	LQ 1976	E. share 1959	E. share 1976	LQ 1959	LQ 1976	E. share 1959	E. share 1976	E. share 1959	E. share 1976
104.5	106.1	32.8	24.3	107.7	98.4	33.8	22.5	92.8	113.0	29.1	26.0	31.4	22.9
100.4	100.2	11.8	10.5	96.7	90.0	11.4	9.4	82.7	83.3	9.7	8.7	11.8	10.4
94.2	99.1	9.6	14.6	88.2	84.3	9.0	12.4	61.4	59.2	6.3	8.7	10.2	14.7
100.9	100.1	15.3	16.0	101.5	106.1	15.4	17.0	108.1	105.6	16.4	16.9	15.2	16.0
93.3	93.0	4.2	4.0	104.4	109.3	4.7	4.7	88.9	93.0	4.0	4.0	4.5	4.3
102.9	101.5	3.6	6.6	97.1	96.9	3.4	6.3	94.3	90.8	3.3	5.9	3.5	6.5
95.8	93.7	15.7	18.2	94.3	110.6	25.4	21.5	128.9	118.7	21.0	23.1	16.4	19.5
		100.0	100.0			100.0	100.0			100.0	100.0	100.0	100.0

service outlets (Cohen 1979). As Table 5.2 indicates, by 1976 the share of employment in the complex of corporate activities among Size 1 SMSAs had caught up with that of manufacturing.

Agglomeration tendencies have been important not simply among producer services and corporate headquarters or divisional head offices, but also between these services and a host of private sector consumer services, public sector, and nonprofit services. Specialty retail stores, restaurants, theaters, universities, major hospitals, and specialized governmental services have tended to locate more frequently in large places because of the larger markets to be served, while corporations and their attendant producer service firms were drawn to larger places, in turn, because of the larger support system of consumer and not-for-profit services which they found there.

Such considerations seem to explain the slightly above-average concentration of some of the residentiary services observable among Size 1 and 2 SMSAs from the data presented in Table 5.2. Among these, those services which are more innovative are more likely to be found in the center of very large markets where firms enjoy their best opportunities for access to and success with customers.

Manufacturing. The location of manufacturing employment has demonstrated exactly the reverse of the trend exhibited by the export services. This is indeed a very important dimension of the transformational process at work throughout the system of cities. Manufacturing has steadily moved away from the larger urban centers toward smaller ones. The process is somewhat more complicated than that revealed by the data, however.

Since before World War II, the locational economics of production facilities has gone through three, *often overlapping*, phases: a "suburbanization" phase, a "regionalization" phase, and a "decentralization" phase.[6] The first phase was characterized by a move away from the central cities of the old traditional manufacturing centers of the northeast and north central regions toward their suburbs. Examples of suburban manufacturing development abound, including the development of the northern Jersey petrochemical industry (away from New York City) and that of the Dearborn automobile industry (away from Detroit). Such decentralization is part of the explanation of the suburbanization process in the United States which began before World War II.

The second phase was marked by the move of manufacturing toward the Sunbelt metropolitan centers. The development of military and aerospace industries is characteristic of this phase (Los Angeles, Atlanta, San Diego) as is, to some extent, the early growth of the electronics industry (San José, Phoenix, Dallas). In cases such as the relocation of the textile industry away from New England to the southern Piedmont region, this phase of regionalization goes back to a much earlier period.

The third and most recent phase has been characterized by a general move away from large centers — almost regardless of regional considerations — toward smaller metropolitan centers and even nonmetropolitan counties. This is best seen in the electrical machinery industry, where the most recent trend has been to expand in places such as Colorado Springs (Digital Equipment), Tucson, and rural Vermont (General Electric); but it is happening in other industries as well: Volkswagen in New Stanton, Pennsylvania, and Cummins Engine and TRW in Jamestown, New York. Meanwhile, cities such as Atlanta or Los Angeles, whose manufacturing had grown substantially until the late 1960s, experienced dramatic losses in the early 1970s.

These trends have come about as a result of either the locational decisions of the new industries (where they chose to locate when they first started) or the relocation of some of the production establishments of older industries, as in the auto industry.

Three economic factors appear to have overwhelmingly determined this behavior: transportation, technology, and blue collar labor cost.[7] The construction of the interstate highway system, the rise of the trucking industry, the parallel decline of the railroads, and the increased routinization and simplification of production processes by way of machinery constitute probably the most important transportation and technological factors that explain the changing geography of manufacturing facilities. In addition, labor cost considerations have often been at the root of this relocation process, since manufacturers have fled high blue collar labor costs and workplace restrictions imposed in certain areas by unionization and labor unrest (Gordon 1978).

Regional Shifts: Sunbelt versus Snowbelt

The analysis presented in the previous paragraphs has pointed to new locational tendencies in manufacturing and the services and to some of the factors that have influenced this behavior. What it has not indicated clearly is the relative importance — and the changes in the relative importance — of the various industry groups and subgroups in the economies of individual cities and regions. These are treated briefly in this and the following sections: first, in terms of the regional shifts demonstrated by the U.S. economy over the past two decades and second, in terms of the restructuring of the system of cities.

During the 1960s, one out of every five jobs added were in the manufacturing sector, with the Sunbelt capturing a disproportionately large share.[8] This differential growth and the growth of some related intermediate support services in the Sunbelt contributed to the very rapid development of the southern urban system during that decade. During the 1970s, manufacturing employment declined drastically in the Snowbelt, but remained virtually constant in the Sunbelt. For the economy as a whole, one out of every four jobs added was in the complex of corporate services.

The record shows, however, that once adjusted for differentials in growth rates between the two regions, the Snowbelt has consistently been successful in capturing more than its share of the growth of the complex of corporate activities and other key services, although these jobs have landed largely in selected urban centers.

In short, growth and transformation came hand in hand. While the opening up of the South as both a consumer market and a site for production resulted in substantial numbers of job openings in manufacturing production, the distributive services, and the consumer-oriented service areas, it put ever greater requirements on intermediate services necessary to coordinate the whole economy. The impact of *growth* was felt disproportionately by the Sunbelt, but the impact of the *service transformation* affected both regions — with the Snowbelt reinforcing its comparative advantage in the key intermediate services.

The New Urban Hierarchy

To capture the impact of both growth and transformation on individual cities of the urban system, Noyelle and Stanback have devised a simple typology of the 140 largest SMSAs for 1976 in their *Economic Transformation in American Cities* (forthcoming). This typology classifies places on the basis of special strength in their export base, as measured by employment in the major industry groups used throughout this volume and other indicators of structure.

This typology yields eleven types of places (Appendix Table A.2) that can be reorganized simply into five major groupings.

1. *The Nodal Centers* (36 centers) include three subgroups of places that may be generally described as "national," "regional," or "subregional" centers. They are characterized by economic bases both strongly specialized and diversified in the distributive services and in the complex of corporate activities, although the influence of the latter declines as one moves down the population size hierarchy of nodal centers. This finding is consistent with our earlier observation regarding the importance of the factor of size of urban places in the location of corporate headquarters and producer-service firms. On the other hand, recent trends indicate that wholesaling, warehousing, or transportation functions have tended to play a relatively more important role in medium size or smaller nodal centers. This, we suspect, is a result of the interplay between changing transportation and technology in the distributive services (e.g. the shift from rail to trucks, the new emphasis on containerization).

The three layers of nodal centers thus simply reflect the size and degree of specialization permitted by the market areas each serves. Perhaps the most significant characteristics of the *four national nodal centers* (New York, Los Angeles, Chicago, and San Francisco) is their huge banking capacity. This banking capacity is accompanied by a great intensity and diversity in the producer-service area, advertising (overwhelmingly dominated by New York), auditing, consulting, investment banking, and so forth (Cohen 1979). These four national centers are also the home of close to 200 of the 500 largest industrial corporations (including 100 in New York itself). Among them are corporations that are likely to be involved in international trade or worldwide manufacturing operations, which need specialized, international expertise from producer-service firms (Conservation of Human Resources 1977).

The *nineteen regional centers* (for example, Philadelphia, Boston, Cleveland, Houston, and Atlanta) are somewhat less sophisticated in the range of producer services they offer. Their primary role is to provide a base from which large corporations can administer their industrial and commercial operations in the main regional markets of the economy. Among these centers are likely to be found the regional offices of almost every large corporation operating continentwide or the headquarters of firms less internationalized than those found in the national centers but still closely tied to large regional consumer markets (e.g., large food companies, large retail or transportation firms). These centers are often characterized by large airport capacity and extensive airline connections — requirements for businessmen who must be able to move quickly between the corporation's regional offices and its home office.

The *thirteen subregional centers* (e.g., Memphis, Omaha, Charlotte, and Des Moines) offer a less diversified version of the kind of producer services provided in the regional centers, but stand out by their strong involvement in the distributive services. One interesting characteristic of these cities is that they often remain closely tied to agricultural markets.

2. *The Functional Nodal Centers* (24 centers) are a somewhat peculiar breed and do not fit well within the conventional model of the urban hierarchy. To use Dunn's terminology (1980), they are largely "off-centered." In employment terms, they stand out in terms of their strength, both in manufacturing-production and as sites for the central administrative and related facilities of the large corporations. Although they can be quite large population-wise (many of them approach the size of the regional and subregional

nodal centers), they have little involvement with regional consumer markets. They are characterized by the articulation of administration, research, and production functions in selected, well-defined complexes of industries (e.g., Detroit in the automobile industry, Pittsburgh in steel, San José in electronics, Rochester in scientific and office equipment, Greensboro-High Point in textiles and furnitures, and so forth). Typically, the firms headquartered in these places are not directly tied to consumer markets.

These cities are usually very strong centers of R&D in their industry, and their production facilities are closely tied to this research and development effort (test facilities for new products, for new manufacturing methods, etc.). While many of these centers have lost production employment as a result of adjustments to changes in technology or competitive environments, they seem to provide relatively stable employment for blue collar workers *once these readjustments have taken place,* because of the close relationship between development and production.

3. *The Government and Education Places* (20 centers) include two somewhat different groups: government places (e.g., Albany, Austin, Sacramento, and Washington, D.C.) which are usually state capitols (where the seat of state government is not already found in a nodal center); and education centers (e.g., New Haven or Ann Arbor) where large universities have prospered outside the environment of large cities. They are characterized by an overconcentration of employment in the government and/or nonprofit sectors. State government places have tended to prosper, in part because of the rising importance of the public sector in the larger economy and in part because the growth of the public sector has largely tended to occur at the state level over the past ten years or so. Education centers have been strongly influenced by changing forces of growth brought about by dramatic shifts in demographic composition and the increased emphasis on specialized higher education.

4. *The Production Centers* (48 centers) include three groups of places: manufacturing (e.g., Buffalo, Youngstown, Reading, and Greenville-Spartanburg), industrial-military (San Diego and Norfolk), and mining centers (Bakersfield and

Charleston, West Virginia). In employment terms they are characterized respectively by an overconcentration of employment in manufacturing, in government (mostly military related, e.g. army, navy, or air force bases, shipyards, arsenals, etc.) or in mining. Industrial-military places enjoyed fairly rapid development from the 1940s until the 1960s because of their direct linkage to the various war and defense efforts (ordinance, shipbuilding, aerospace).

By comparison with the functional nodal centers, the production centers are more likely to be engaged in run-of-the-mill production and to have very little involvement in the planning, administration, or research and development of the industry in which they specialize.

5. *The Residential Centers* (12 centers). These centers include two sets of places: the suburban metropolises of the very large nodal centers (Nassau-Suffolk and Long Branch around New York, Anaheim and Riverside around Los Angeles, possibly Vallejo near San Francisco) and a set of resort-retirement centers (West Palm Beach, Orlando, or Las Vegas) that have sprung up in the postwar era under the combined effects of rising consumerism (strongly influenced by higher discretionary income, paid vacations) and generalized retirement benefits.

Growth and Transformation

Table 5.3 shows a detailed record of growth performance of these 140 largest SMSAs by type, size, and region. For this purpose, the 140 SMSAs have been divided into five equal quintiles (28 places each) on the basis of rates of employment growth in each place between 1959 and 1976.

On the whole, the Sunbelt SMSAs have tended to grow faster than their northern counterparts. This is consistent with our earlier finding regarding regional shifts, and simply states that the Sunbelt urban system grew to catch up with that of the Snowbelt. The fact that Sunbelt places tended to be relatively smaller than northern places, both at the beginning and at the end of the long 1959– 1976 period, translated into somewhat faster growth among size 2 and size 4 SMSAs, as compared to size 1 and size 3 SMSAs.

When analyzed by types, places exhibited somewhat different growth tendencies. Government and education places on the one hand and residential resort and retirement centers on the other were consistently among some of the fastest growing places.

Among the manufacturing, industrial-military, and mining places, only the industrial-military exhibited relatively rapid growth, a reflection of the importance of the growth of the industrial-military complex throughout the postwar era. The slow rate of growth among manufacturing centers, on the contrary, reflected the setbacks of many basic U.S. industries in the most recent period (automobile, automobile parts, tires, steel, etc.) and the trend toward internationalization of production, which affected these places most particularly.

The growth performance of the functional nodal centers reflects the influence of the same trends, although among these places the process of retrenchment was usually not as drastic as it was in some of the manufacturing centers. This seems related to the fact that in such centers firms tended to have heavier investments in their production facilities because of the link between research and development and experimental production. As a result employment appears to be less subject to large-scale layoffs during cyclical downturns. This observation applies not only to functional nodal centers, but also to a substantial number of nodal centers where the same linkage between production and research obtains in certain industries. Analysis has shown that it is primarily in northern centers that the relationship between research and development and nonroutine production is to be found (Malecki 1979). Most importantly, this applies to a number of industries traditionally associated with postwar growth and the rise of the Sunbelt (aerospace, ordnance, energy, electronics, computers, scientific equipment). While there are noticeable Sunbelt exceptions (San José or Dallas in electronics, Denver and Houston in energy, etc.), it seems that northern metropolises have, on the whole, been quite successful in holding their own and preserving the best, most skill-intensive part of the manufacturing production and development processes, while southern places have tended to capture employment in more routine production.

Table 5.3 Distribution of 1976 Size 1 through Size 4 SMSAs by Size, Quintile of Growth (1959–76), Type, and Region

SMSAs by size and by quintile of growth	Nat'l Nodal	Reg'l Nodal	Subreg'l Nodal	Funct'l Nodal	Govt, (& Ed)	Ed'n (& Mfg)	Resid'l	Resort-Retir't	Mfg	Ind'l-Mltry	Mining	All Places
Very rapid												
Size 1		2										2
Size 2		4		1			1	1				7 28
Size 3			1				1	2	1			5
Size 4					5	1		3	1	3	1	14
Rapid												
Size 1					1		1					2
Size 2		1						1		1		3 28
Size 3			6	2	1			1		1		11
Size 4			2		3			1		5	1	12
Moderate												
Size 1	1	1										2
Size 2		4										4 28
Size 3			1	3					1	1		6
Size 4			1	3	1	1			7	1	2	16
Slow												
Size 1	1	1		1								3
Size 2		1		2								3 28
Size 3			1	5					2			8
Size 4			1	2	2				8		1	14

	1	2	3	4	5	6	7	8	9	10	11	Total
Very slow												
Size 1	2		2		0		3				2	8
Size 2	4		1					1	5		2	2 28
Size 3								3		2		10
Size 4	1		1	1				3				8
Very rapid and rapid	0	Snow: 0 Sun: 7	9 Snow: 0 Sun: 9	3 Snow: 1 Sun: 2	10 Snow: 3 Sun: 7	1 Snow: 1 Sun: 0	3 Snow: 2 Sun: 1	9 Snow: 0 Sun: 9	2 Snow: 0 Sun: 2	10 Snow: 0 Sun: 10	2 Snow: 0 Sun: 2	56 Snow: 7 Sun: 49
Moderate	1	5 Snow: 3 Sun: 2	2 Snow: 0 Sun: 3	6 Snow: 3 Sun: 3	1 Snow: 0 Sun: 1	1 Snow: 0 Sun: 1	0	0	8 Snow: 5 Sun: 3	2 Snow: 0 Sun: 2	2 Snow: 0 Sun: 2	28 Snow: 13 Sun: 15
Slow and very slow	3 Snow: 2 Sun: 1	7 Snow: 7 Sun: 0	2 Snow: 1 Sun: 1	15 Snow: 15 Sun: 0	4 Snow: 4 Sun: 0	3 Snow: 3 Sun: 0	0	0	19 Snow: 15 Sun: 4	3 Snow: 2 Sun: 1		56 Snow: 49 Sun: 7
Total	4	19	13	24	15	9	3	9	29	12	7	140
Snow	2	10	3	19	7	2	2	0	20	0	2	69
Sun	2	9	10	5	8	9	1	9	9	12	5	71

Note: Snowbelt includes cities in New England, Mid-East, Great Lakes, and Plains; Sunbelt includes cities in Southeast, Southwest, Rocky Mountain, and Far West.

Source: From T. Noyelle and T. Stanback, *Economic Transformation in American Cities* (forthcoming).

Among the nodal centers, the regional and subregional centers tended to display higher rates of growth than the national centers. A more detailed examination of this trend indicates that growth has favored especially the regional centers, which were reinforcing their strength in the complex of corporate activities, while the subregional centers as a whole appear to have fared less well. Here we see several factors at work. First, the unfavorable price structure of the very large centers at the turn of the 1970s (cost of land, rents, labor costs, etc.) was a strong incentive for large firms that did not really need to be headquartered in these centers (i.e. the less internationalized firms) to relocate in regional centers (Conservation of Human Resources 1977). Second, the very strong merger movement of the 1960s and 1970s transformed a number of large, but formerly regional, corporations into firms now concerned with nationwide markets (Cohen 1979). This forced many such corporations to revamp their organizations and to adopt regional-divisional structures calling for major regional head office facilities in key regional nodal centers. Third, the growth and increasing maturity of regional markets provided a demand for sophisticated business and financial services, which was of sufficient size to permit services that previously had been available only in the very largest cities to be offered in regional centers. These trends clearly boosted the development of the Sunbelt's regional nodal centers (Atlanta, Denver, Phoenix, Dallas, Houston, etc.), and brought about a sorting out of roles among older, Snowbelt, regional nodal centers. In the process, some of the Snowbelt centers managed successfully to reposition themselves (e.g., Boston, Philadelphia, Cincinnati, or Columbus), while others had problems keeping up with their neighbors (certainly Detroit or Pittsburgh, but perhaps also places such as Baltimore or Cleveland). In the latter case, these northern centers were usually reduced to playing a more secondary role as functional nodal centers.

**Concluding Remarks: The Impact of the Transformation
on Urban Economies**
To evaluate the impact of the transformation of the urban system would require a more elaborate analysis than the one

which can be presented in this short concluding section. A few issues deserve to be brought to the reader's attention, however.

First, the shift to services has been somewhat unsatisfactory in employment terms. While this has been due in part to the strains that have resulted from the sharp increases in women's participation in the labor force, there is evidence that the economy as a whole did not succeed as well in the recent decade (in terms of the rate of expansion and the absolute number of jobs created) as it had during the 1960s. In many SMSAs, unemployment rates have remained quite high, reflecting, at least in part, employment problems inherent in the shift to services.

Second, there is evidence that the loss of good middle income manufacturing jobs has had adverse income effects in many cities. This trend, however, appears to have affected different cities and different socioeconomic groups in different ways. Both Stanback and Noyelle (1981) and Harrison and Hill (1979) have found that where cities shifted sharply toward a service employment base, the loss of middle income jobs appeared to be the most dramatic. As observed earlier, many of the new jobs in the services are low pay and have been taken by women, often as secondary workers in the family. Where a doubling-up of earning power occurs or where the breadwinners are highly paid professionals or executives, family earnings are relatively high. But where the individual or entire family must rely on low-pay service jobs, frequently on a part-time basis, earnings are low.

Third, the most troublesome aspect of the transformation in this respect seems to lie among minority workers. There is strong evidence (Stanback and Noyelle 1981) that some members of the minority populations — particularly black males — who were likely to play only a peripheral role in the blue collar economy — may be in the process of becoming left out of the white collar economy.

What may be most important to understand is the fact that the shift to the services has largely been an *urban-based* transformation associated with a rapid and massive transformation from blue collar to white collar forms of work. New forms of discipline, new social orientations, new skills, and new training have had to be provided by the family, by the schools and, more broadly speaking, by the social system. Clearly, local government has had a major role to play in this endeavor. The extent to which local institutions have adapted to the change and promoted rather than hindered this transformation of work and work values may well have been one of the most important factors in achieving successful urban transformations. Given that the location of corporate producer services has been very sensitive to the urban concentration of the professional and technical segments of the labor force (and vice versa), one may argue that the extent to which individual local governments have striven to promote the development of these strategic worker groups may contribute to explaining much of the success of individual cities.

At the same time, however, if the analysis of the transformation of the urban system presented in this chapter provides an indication of future trends, it may well be that the most innovative dimensions of the transformation at work — which features the development of new services and the birth of new service-based firms — has been and will remain strongly restricted to those metropolitan centers that are already well established as part of the service economy. This may make it increasingly difficult for other centers to break out of the more secondary role they play in today's economy.

Notes

[1]See *New York Times*, March 16, 1980 and March 23, 1980, cited in Chapter 2.

[2]Much of the presentation that follows is based on findings from Noyelle's and Stanback's ongoing research on the transformation of the U.S. urban system (1981 forthcoming).

[3]For a review of the limitations of this concept, see Watkins 1980.

[4]The location quotient is the ratio of the average share of employment in a given industry in a given size group of places to the corresponding share for the industry in the national economy. By definition the location quotient for each industry for the nation is 1.0 (or 100.0 once multiplied by the appropriate factor).

[5]Employment in the producer services and in the central administrative offices of firms combined.

[6]For a detailed analysis of these three phases, see *The President's National Urban Policy Report*, 1980.

[7]Ultimately, these same factors explain most of the recent development of the internationalization process of U.S. manufacturing.

[8]For a more detailed discussion of the rise of the Sunbelt see, for example, Sternlieb and Hughes (1975), Perry and Watkins (1977), or Mollenkopf (1979).

[9]Size 1 through Size 4 SMSAs.

6. Building Blocks for New Bridges Between Theory and Policy

The Intersect of Data and Theory

A reconceptualization of the transformation undergone by the U. S. economy in recent decades begins not with imagining a new set of disembodied abstractions nor with bewailing the lack of data, but with confronting the several puzzling observations emerging from available empirical evidence that current theories cannot explain. Early on in this project, several puzzles became apparent:

1. The large and persistent gap in productivity between manufacturing and services measured by conventional methods

2. The much greater significance of services in employment terms than in income or output terms; similarly, the more rapid growth of services employment than of services output

3. Recent, but still not conclusive, evidence that the rate of productivity increase in services is rising and that the productivity gap between manufacturing and services may be diminishing

4. Evidence that the growth of producer services has been much more significant than previous studies had indicated

5. Evidence of the rising scale of service firms — somewhat of an anomaly when compared to productivity observations

6. A puzzle implied by 1. above: that the growth of the services sector seems to contradict an economic "law" that

faster growth in employment should be accompanied by faster growth in productivity

7.   Evidence that, contrary to conventional belief, a significant portion of the services sector is not merely "residentiary" or "nonbasic" activity, but is export-oriented and locationally sensitive to city size or other indicators of urbanization

8.   Indications that services have grown faster or that a higher proportion of their growth has been "captured" in cities and regions outside of the old industrial belt

9.   Indications from project case studies and the literature that services play a fundamental "binding," integrative, and developmental role both within large organizations and within the larger economy

10.   Evidence that the transformation has gone on (and probably began) *within* manufacturing, in that the growth of service-like employment (involving various types of non-production workers) within that sector has proceeded steadily for a long time, in spite of its overall employment decline

11.   Preliminary indications that the fastest growing services in the private sector are those which are the newer, more information-rich service specializations

12.   Indications that the growing predominance of services in the economy has been accompanied by significant changes in economic organization and the nature of work

It is not necessarily apparent that each of these, taken individually, is a "puzzle"; rather, all of them together represent a set of puzzles which fit uneasily, if at all, within the rubric of received economic theory. For instance, items 1 and 2, relating to productivity, are puzzling in light of observations 3, 5, 6, 7, 9 and 10. Furthermore, the fact that these observations are difficult to explain in light of received theories is puzzling in itself.

Lagging Perceptions of New Realities

Current economic theory is not a suitable framework for trying to explain a long-run, evolutionary process of development. The main body of economic thinking is still too largely static, equilibrial, and short term in its time horizon, even though considerable progress has been made in the analysis of economic dynamics. The body of knowledge labeled "economic development" is still largely focused on explicating the transformations of the so-called "LDCs" — less developed countries — not the transformation of advanced industrial economies. Partly as a result, attempts to explain the transformation of the U. S. economy are characterized by vague, descriptive language and the persistence of a number of "myths," including those pointed to earlier.

The nonrigorous, mythical flavor of many explanations, and the fact that these have stayed in good currency for so long in spite of contrary indications, is understandable if one considers that the economy is either at or just past a threshold in a long-run transition. At such an historical juncture it is common for people to perceive what is happening in terms of the "models" or "mental maps" characteristic of the stage of development that is being superseded. Thus, the discourse on the services economy has, so far, largely been obscured by concepts, models, and categories that were tailored to explain the behavior of an economy dominated by the factory.

This is even more a problem for economic policy than it is for economic theory. Once a set of interrelated ideas comes into good currency in the world of policy, it takes on a life of its own. This problem was recognized by Keynes in his famous remark that most policymakers are "the slaves of some defunct economist." This is also understandable on the basis of what we know about behavior. People are generally risk-averse, and they especially loathe uncertainty. At a time of transition, therefore, they will gravitate to familiar theories rather than face uncomfortable facts. The set of ideas associated with a dominant pattern of development, in diffusing through a society, becomes so ingrained that most people are not conscious of their intellectual heritage. Consequently, most people, including most intellectuals, feel only a vague sense of disquiet when the dynamics of development begin to suggest a pattern that is not quite congruent with the mental map they carry about in their heads. Most people, therefore, will continue to act and set policy on the basis of their mindset, as the new pattern of development comes only slowly into view.

This problem — the old policy remedies undermined by a

mismatch between old theory and new patterns of development — is very much in evidence at the present time. One sees it in subnational economic development policies that persist in focusing on manufacturing and ignoring services, policies grounded in a simplistic "economic base" theory of development. One sees it in short-sighted "proposition 13" – type fiscal policies at all levels which, by taking a simple-minded "meat ax" approach to budgeting, ignore the potential for increasing the productivity of public services. One sees it in one of the last of the great "cottage industries," higher education, characterized by a lack of specialization in some respects and overspecialization in others, both detrimental to the advancement of knowledge. One sees it, too, in the mindset of business which, by and large, has not been able to reconceptualize an outdated, artificial dichotomy between public and private, or between manufacturing and services.

The task of reformulating economic policies at all levels is too urgent to wait until the theorists are through constructing a new framework to match a new reality. More likely, the obverse occurs: scholars set about explaining a new reality only long after it has evolved. Ideally, the tasks of reconstructing theory, pursuing empirical investigations, and reconstituting policies should proceed in tandem, each feeding the other. The reformation of policy can provide useful hints for theory and investigation. In a period of transition, practitioners faced with concrete dilemmas will experiment with what might appear, superficially, to be ad hoc solutions to new problems. For observers whose minds are alert to the significance of innovations, however, these will provide valuable clues to the kinds of economic behavior and organization that are likely to emerge from the transition.

Reconceptualization: The Building Blocks of a Dynamic Framework

Progress in reconceptualizing the transformation of the U. S. economy will be made only to the extent that investigators can delineate several dynamic processes and integrate them into an overall framework that fits the stylized facts and patterns of development in an advanced industrial economy. The key word is *dynamic*. Past studies of the growth of services have relied heavily on conventional economic concepts and a fundamentally static framework — price and income elasticities of demand or supply, and production functions. The concepts themselves are not necessarily static, but they have been used in a static way.

There has been little attempt to probe beneath the surface of the concepts to see to what extent they may reflect more basic, structural factors at work. For instance, the income elasticity of demand was a major explanatory factor tested by Fuchs (1968) in his analysis of services growth. His statistical analysis, however, could not distinguish this factor from "urbanization." Some attention to the hint in the data — that the structure of the urban environment might be a basic influence on services growth — would have opened up a new vista for analysis. A lack of attention to other aspects of structure also led Fuchs to underestimate the importance of producer services and large corporations in the transformation of the U. S. economy. The key word here is *structure,* meaning primarily the structure of production along two dimensions: spatial and organizational.

Attention to structure and attention to dynamics necessarily go hand in hand. Dynamic behavior is conditioned by existing structures, and various types of dynamic interactions can gradually alter structural attributes. Wilbur Thompson's (1965) theory of urban economic development, for instance, highlights the significance of the initial advantages of cities, in terms of their infrastructure and services-base, as a major influence on the subsequent evolution of their industry structure. In a more recent comprehensive study, Dunn (1980) documents how the structure of the U. S. urban system has evolved in recent decades, in a way consistent both with Thompson's framework and with Dunn's own, which places heavy emphasis on the structure of basic networks. At the intraregional level, Bearse (1977) demonstrates the preponderant influence of structural features of "initial advantage" for the development and diffusion of new economic activities. These are only a few of the many studies that demonstrate the interrelationship between structural attributes and dynamic behavior.

Our efforts at reconceptualization have helped to identify

and describe some of the main dynamic processes at work in the transformation, although not to link them up into an overall model. With respect to the latter, one should note that it is neither feasible nor appropriate to anticipate a complete quantitative framework. A truly dynamic process of transformation necessarily has many qualitative elements (Georgescu-Roegen 1972) and needs to be discussed at several levels. Our thinking coalesces around several "building blocks," which at some point might be integrated into an overall framework.

Block A.   Networks: Transportation and Communications. From the beginning of economic history, innovations in transportation and communications have had a fundamental influence on the industrial, spatial, and organizational structure of the economy. One need only tick off a few obvious examples to realize how seemingly limited innovations may portend major changes in economy and society: the stirrup (horse cavalry), the compass and chronometer (merchant shipping), the telegraph (integration of financial markets), the railroad (spatial concentration of growth), and the automobile (spatial deconcentration of growth). Present developments are no exception. Low-cost computing and telecommunications technology promises to force major adaptations in most aspects of our political economy. Economically, a basic effect of these innovations is to increase market size by breaking down local market barriers, integrating local markets, and facilitating creation of new markets. Simultaneously, these innovations increase the density, speed, and quality of information flows, which further increases the potential rate of technical progress and the diffusion of innovations. The latter also increase the desire and scope for specialization and differentiation at all levels, as new knowledge spreads and perception of opportunities increases. Other implications were mentioned above, and will appear in the context of the building blocks to follow.

Contrary to superficial judgment, the increasing size of markets and organizations introduces more, not less, uncertainty and disequilibrium tendencies into economic systems at both the macro and micro levels. The increasing complexity of the system makes economic management at all levels problematic. In the business world, oligopolistic competition is more intense, and the uncertainties greater than perhaps many realize, especially in markets which are tending to be worldwide in scope. Size, of course, is no more an "independent" variable than any of the others in our building block scheme. Everything is related to everything else (which says something about the difficulties of "modeling" the system).

Size of organizations and markets are enhanced by the increasing speed, scope, sophistication, and integration of transportation and communications networks (Block A) and urbanization (Block C). Simultaneously, these also increase the speed, quantity, and quality of information flows, and thus the speed at which shocks and innovations are transmitted through the economic system. This, in turn, increases uncertainty and the likelihood of disequilibrium-dynamic tendencies. The latter, in turn, has the consequence of further enhancing the tendencies for increases in size, as organizations of all types merge or diversify in order to better deal with the uncertainties in their environment. (Again, for the largest organizations, the relevant "environment" is worldwide.)

For the largest organizations, however, there is a thin line between competitive strategies that help firms adapt to uncertainty, and strategies that help firms to achieve some control over the relevant environment. Strategies of the latter type, which permit large firms to achieve "micro-stability," may reduce the rate of progress of the overall economy and ultimately increase macro-level *in*-stability (Klein 1977).The largest economic organization is, of course, government. The increasing size of government can be seen, in part, as a response to rising scale and complexity of the rest of the economic system. Government provides some of the most basic services that bind the system together. The increasing scope of government, however, increases the complexity of the environment for business. Thus, in several respects, the strategic interaction between firms and their environment is a matter of central concern for both theory and policy, one which directly implicates a rising role for services and increasing services specialization.

Block B.   Specialization and Integration. In highlighting the structure of production earlier, a key consideration was the increasing size of markets and organizations. Increasing size requires major, qualitative adaptations in the structures of both markets and organizations. One obvious consequence is increasing scope for specialization and differentiation. These tendencies can proceed only so far, however, before new structures or structural adaptations are required to provide some integration among the increasingly specialized or differentiated parts of a growing system. Thus, for instance, increasing diversification of business enterprise must sooner or later call forth new headquarters services or reorganization to provide effective integration of various divisions, else the firm may find itself in severe difficulty (as did many thrown-together conglomerates formed in the late 1960s).

Block C.   Urbanization. During the manufacturing stage of development, increasing urbanization went hand-in-hand with increasing articulation of transportation/communications networks and increasing firm/market size. As Pred (1966) has shown, these three major factors defined a dynamic inter-active pattern of development in which each reinforced the other in a cumulative way. As a result, one observed, for at least 150 years up to about 1950, steadily increasing urbanization, industrialization, and scale in the U. S. economy. A critical mediating factor in this pattern was the creation and exploitation of economies of scale, where scale economies should be interpreted broadly, rather than narrowly, to encompass the economies realizable through utilization of any type of fixed, overhead resources. Thus, what economists refer to as "localization," "agglomeration," and "urbanization" economies are simple generalizations of the basic scale economies concept.

Perhaps the most basic sort of fixed resources are cities. As such, the city, especially the large city, facilitates at a macro scale the process of "diversification from points of common cost" that Penrose (1959) emphasizes is so important in the development of firms. The city can be viewed as a bundle of relatively fixed resources of tremendous variety, so that the utilization of its resources is likewise possessed of great variety and mutability. The fundamental resource is information. Indeed, there have been attempts to rank cities in terms of their stocks of information resources (Sanuki 1970). In Simon's (1957) terms, cities are environments "rich with clues." The depth and variety of urban resources can also be measured in terms of greater shares of relatively fixed human resources, basic infrastructure, and diverse services. This is an environment that, simultaneously, generates and ameliorates uncertainty. Every shock, innovation, fad, or fashion either originates or is transmitted through the urban nodes in the transport and communications networks. The large city environment, as Meier (1962) emphasized, is a "make or break" environment, where institutional, product, and behavioral innovations can gestate at relatively low cost. Indeed, several studies have shown that the incidence of innovation (measured in alternative ways) varies positively with city size. Thus it is no surprise that our empirical results show that specialization in the most innovative and sophisticated producer and consumer services tends to correlate positively with size of urban area. Cities are the sites where the dynamic processes of specialization and differentiation of both products and services via market size are most clearly apparent.[1] Likewise, the integrative role of various services is most clearly apparent in urban settings.

Block D. Knowledge. Following Abramovitz (1972), we cite the systematic application of science and technology in every field of human endeavor as one of the most fundamental factors driving the transformation of the U. S. economy. Kuznets was quite apt in labeling this an "autonomous" factor. This label simply highlights the fact that the application has become institutionalized in such a way that growth in the stock of knowledge is at least partly (though not entirely) independent of demand factors; that the "supply side" is fundamental in the dynamics of the system. Stigler (1956) recognized this when he pointed to a dynamic interaction between the supply of knowledge and the demand for knowledge. This is a situation, he noted, where supply creates its own demand, in a cumulatively reinforcing way. With respect to services, one should note the increasing application of "soft" technologies in business and government, as science-based analytical tools are applied to problems of management, policy, and human behavior.

This aspect of dynamics highlights the human resources factor in the transformation of the economy. Ultimately, as Theodore Schultz observed in the German "miracle" following World War II, the ability of a country (or an organization) to recover from disaster is dependent upon the stock of knowledge embodied in its workforce. The ability of an already large, advanced economy or organization to maintain dynamic behavior, however, is a never ending problem — perhaps *the* problem facing highly developed societies. Organization theorists point to ever present tendencies toward "institutional entropy," by which organizations of all types, especially large organizations, are constantly in danger of hardening of the arteries.

Block E. Stage of Development. The introduction defined "stage of development" along dimensions that included activity (the nature of work) and organization (structure of production). One's intuitive hunch that the U.S. economy is now at a stage of development that is qualitatively different from the manufacturing stage is confirmed by noting the very different forms of activity and organization that characterize the "leading edge" (fastest growing) sectors of the U.S. economy, as well as the radical transformation within "manufacturing" itself. Data do not indicate a discontinuity in the U.S. path of development, but there are ample indications that we are well into a new stage. As with most innovations in a highly urbanized society, the signs and signals of transition are seen first in the largest cities. Pred (1965) observes that manufacturing activities stopped expanding in the larger cities around about 1919. For the U.S. economy as a whole, it appears that the early fifties marked something of a transition, in that manufacturing employment has been in secular decline ever since. If one views the process of development as being a gradual process of innovation and diffusion, then one should expect (1) to see an uneven development process in the spatial dimension but (2) not necessarily observe sharp discontinuities over time. In other words, at the macro-level, the manifestations of a new stage of development will gradually become clear only over a long period of time. The only certainty is that the transformation will ultimately be wholesale, marked by qualitative as well as quantitative changes in all spheres of economy and society: consumer behavior, the nature of work, economic organizaton, and spatial organization, among others. The rates of adaptation of different sectors and organizations in the economy will differ widely. The process by which the ramifications of a new stage of development spread through the society, again, is a disequilibrium-dynamic process.[2] Whether one labels the new stage "the service economy," the "information economy," the "knowledge economy," or, simply, the "new industrial economy" is, at this point, a matter of taste.

A corollary of the stage of development thesis is that other time-dependent processes noted by "age" and "product cycle" become even more problematic. The age of organizations and cities has been recognized as a serious problem in their adaptation to new socio-economic circumstances. The concept of age has little to do with calendar years. It relates, fundamentally, to the issue cited above: the ability of organizations (including cities and governmental units) to maintain dynamic, adaptive modes of behavior. A basic indicator of age is the extent to which organizations are overspecialized or overinvested in types of activity, types of technology, or capital stocks that were characteristic of an earlier stage or cycle of development. Another is the atrophy of entrepreneurship. Thus, adaptability is highly constrained and/or lacks leadership. We observe, for instance, higher growth rates of new services and new technology-based industries in cities that did not become overspecialized in manufacturing (Mollenkopf 1979). Similarly, a host of studies documents that small or new business organizations are more innovative than large. Most large businesses have learned (sometimes the hard way) that overspecialization in a few "maturing" product lines spells serious problems somewhere down the line.

Block F.   Government. In economic theory, there is a concept of "externalities" (or "spillovers"), representing mainly social costs or benefits, which provides a textbook rationale for governmental provision of goods and services. It is an essentially static concept. It is, moreover, narrowly construed as somewhat of an aberration in what is otherwise thought to be an equilibrial, smoothly adjusting, and efficient economic system. By contrast, a dynamic perspective implicates spillovers as a normal, widespread, and essential feature of an advanced market economy.[3] The significance of spillovers as a dynamic factor, moreover, is most likely increasing, *not* decreasing, with urbanization and the increasing density, speed, and articulation of networks. Spillovers and imbalances are constantly being created in the economy — between cities, regions, sectors, industries, and firms. Opportunities for entrepreneurship are, thereby, constantly being recreated.

This perspective has several implications for government and the evolution of public sector/private sector relationships. Each sector is the source of spillovers that affect the other. The obvious example is the private polluter who imposes social costs on the public; however, either sector can generate public "goods" or public "bads." Private sector research, development, and other activities can and do generate benefits that are not entirely appropriated by the firms which invest their resources. Similarly, ill-conceived government laws and regulations may have adverse "spillover" effects on private business, which are not simply justified by the social costs of business activity, or which have dynamic effects that outweigh static benefits.

These interactions imply a relationship between the sectors that is increasingly one of overlap, interpenetration, and co-mingling of functions and decisions. The boundary between what is private and what is public is increasingly fuzzy. This further implies that continuing effort to redefine sectoral relationships will be part and parcel of the economy's transformation, with major political and ideological overtones. The directions redefinition may take, moreover, will not be simply one way. People in either domain will be willing to intrude on prerogatives that were once thought to be the exclusive concern of the other.

The basic causes of the rise of government in the American economy have been noted elsewhere: two world wars, the breakdown of market economies during the 1930s, the movements for equity or equal opportunity, and so on. A feature and a consequence of this rise has been a reciprocal, intersectoral, cause-and-effect type of relationship helping to fuel the growth of services in the economy. On the one hand, government has grown in response to the social costs and uncertainties of private enterprise. On the other hand, the growing influence of government has led to the growth of private sector services to deal with government and a competitive environment influenced by government.

The growth of government from the 1930s to the present has meant that the public sector is no longer overwhelmingly outsized by the private sector. As a result, a stably unstable relationship between the sectors has developed, not unlike a relationship between duopolists. There is a dynamic tension between the sectors that, at least for several years, will cause the relative size of the sectors to ebb and flow, but within a narrow range. It is not at all likely that the size of the public sector in an advanced economy can be significantly diminished. There are powerful sources of stability in the public sector, generally recognized in the public finance and public administration literature.

Productivity

A Dynamic Framework. The concepts we have been discussing in this chapter seem to be implicated in the problem of productivity. Productivity is perhaps the most complex issue on the nation's policy agenda, not merely because it is central to growth and development, but because it cross-cuts so many other concerns (e.g., inflation and fiscal problems). Perhaps more than any other single concept, understanding the causes of changing productivity is crucial to understanding the transformation of the economy (and vice versa). Productivity is thus a symptomatic concern of both theory and policy. To a greater extent than any other economic problem, the inability of economists to adequately diagnose the sources of productivity (and related problems of inflation) indicates the need for a new theoretical framework that is disequilibrium-dynamic in nature and that links the macro and micro levels of analysis. For these reasons it is à propos to focus on productivity, and the focus will provide an illustration of how our theoretical "building blocks" can help diagnose a policy issue.

The promise of dynamic formulations is most sharply revealed by the failure of static formulations. For years, economists have relied upon a static production function/growth accounting framework in their attempts to identify the

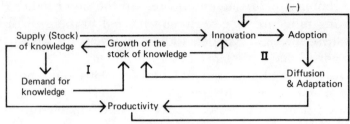

Note: for explanation of symbols I, II, and (−) see text.

Figure 6.1   Flow-Diagram

sources of productivity growth. This line of investigation
seems no longer fruitful, as Denison's (1979) accounting results appear to indicate, or as do a variety of other basic
criticisms of the production function approach (e.g. Thurow
1975; Simon 1979). It has always been a problem with the
production function approach that the most significant factors influencing productivity (innovation, technical progress,
and others implicated in the blocks above) get lumped into a
"residual," which invariably accounts for 60–70 percent of
the variation in productivity. One now finds in Denison's
observations that the residual contribution declined in the late
1970s. The static growth–accounting framework that
provides this provocative observation, however, is quite unable to help explain it. A dynamic framework is sorely needed,
and the energies of the economic research community must
be devoted to the construction and testing of dynamic models,
even if the initial attempts are crude and unsatisfactory.[4]

The dynamic process leading to increases in productivity
can be represented by a flow-diagram, Figure 6.1. The rate of
growth of productivity overall and the differences in productivity between industries and areas depend on the speeds
and lags in this process. Empirical studies (Mansfield 1961;
Davies 1979) show that the lags between innovation, adoption
and diffusion are frequently quite long (10–20 years for
many manufacturing innovations) and vary significantly both
within and between industries. Likewise, productivity measurements differ significantly between sectors, industries,
cities, and regions.

In a competitive environment, gaps and lags in productivity, innovation, and diffusion will themselves tend to spur productivity, innovation, and diffusion as laggard firms, industries, and sectors try to catch up or keep from falling too far behind. This is one reason why the process outlined above is disequilibrium-dynamic: not only is it a process of uneven development, but the nature and extent of the unevenness is itself an influential factor in the economy's transformation. There is no equilibrium; i.e., no ultimate or hypothetical state of the system that is independent of the path of development.

Another reason is that there are cumulative and reinforcing subprocesses. These are the (semiclosed) cycles labelled I and II in Figure 6.1. Each of the arrows denotes a positive cause-effect type of relationship. Cumulative, reinforcing processes are disequilibrium in nature because they give rise to positive, rather than negative, feedback (Maruyama 1963). The exception, denoted (-) above, is the feedback connection between productivity and innovation. Rising productivity and its correlates, rising profitability and discretionary incomes, eventually dampen innovation and related sources of productivity growth, because the incentives to innovate and use resources more efficiently are diminished. Another reason for negative feedback here is that the adjustment costs of continuing to increase productivity at a high rate will at some point begin to rise. Just so much growth and differentiation can be accomodated within a given structure of production before the structure itself must be reorganized. In the medium term, such reorganization will absorb scarce resources, but the reorganized structure will eventually serve as a basis for renewed productivity advance. In addition, the incentive for such advances will also be reestablished as organizations at all levels use up their surpluses and confront real threats to their continuing prosperity (cf. Klein 1977 and 1980).

It is important to note that the speed and other characteristics of subprocesses in the above scheme depend on the structure of the environment in which they occur. Processes of innovation, adoption, and diffusion are facilitated by urbanization and by the growing speed, density, and sophistication of communications and transportation networks, as well as the growth of knowledge. Also, the ability of any subunit in the system to innovate and adapt is constrained by the organization, structures, and investments inherited from a previous stage of development.

Productivity Differentials and Economic Transformation. The scheme outlined above provides at least the beginning of an explanation of (1) why we observe significant productivity differentials among sectors, firms, and cities, and (2) why productivity measurements typically underestimate the actual productivity of a dynamic economy. The problem is simply this: if services are indeed low productivity activities, then a shift in the composition of output toward services implies a somewhat lower growth rate of productivity overall. Fuchs (1977) and Denison (1979) observe that, statistically, the effect is small, perhaps on the order on 0.1 percentage point less in the rate. Yet it is generally acknowledged that the macro-level data on which such estimates are based are flawed by unknown but perhaps significant errors in measuring the productivity of services at the micro level. Therefore, it is important to try to assess the direction of bias at that level. This assessment requires that we distinguish levels from rates and internal from external activities. The productivity of services is underestimated to the extent that services industries are growing faster than others (which they are), are internalized, are intermediate (largely purchased by producers rather than consumers), involve the creation of various types of capital, and involve firm-specific transactions. To this one should add that the productivity of any activity is typically underestimated to the extent that it is innovative. Grilisches (1979), for instance, notes that current statistical methods significantly underestimate the productivity of the computer industry.

Treadway (1968) demonstrates that to the extent that a firm is creating relatively fixed, firm-specific capital (or capacity) as a joint product with its marketable output, its productivity is underestimated. The degree of bias, moreover, will be greater, the greater the rate of growth of the firm and the more its internal capacity building activities are subject to economies of scale.

The linkages and overlap among various facets of productivity measurement become apparent when one notes that productivity measurement in most cases (except for studies based on engineering or other specially collected data) is based on market prices for outputs and inputs. Market prices do not adequately represent "cost" or "value" in situations where markets have not yet or have only partially been established, where the relevant markets are largely internal, or where markets are not reasonably competitive. A major class of situations where these conditions obtain are the early stages of innovation-diffusion processes; e.g., at early phases of product cycles, or at an early stage of development of an entire new industry. In these situations, output markets do not yet exist; they must be created. Likewise, on the input side, appropriate resources are often not available for purchase on open markets; they must be created. The latter considerations embrace both goods and services: for example, new forms of trained labor (human capital) as well as new forms of machinery. IBM and other high technology firms have had themselves to develop much of the sophisticated machinery and trained labor they need to produce and sell their products. Since the appropriate resources cannot be obtained "off the shelf" or on the market, they must usually be developed "in-house," at least initially. The earlier the stage of the innovation-diffusion process, the more likely it is that the relevant resources will be produced internally. Only at a much later stage of development does a large enough pool of the appropriate resources become available and begin to move between firms and industries, so that one can say that a "market" exists and that market prices are beginning to provide a reasonable approximation of the value of these resources in production.[5] Then, market prices for services purchased on external markets provide some approximation to the value of the output. How good or how poor the approximation is cannot be answered without empirical studies of pricing and demand for various producer services, studies that are mostly unavailable. It is possible, for instance, that management services represent a reserve of (otherwise fixed) managerial capacity whose value to firms is not fully measured by consultants' fees.

These considerations highlight the relevance of the "age," "stage," and "product cycle" concepts introduced earlier. The "stage of development" concept is even more broadly implicated. Considered broadly, as sectors, manufacturing and services differ fundamentally with respect to the dimensions cited above: age, stage, internalization, reliance upon human capital, extent of firm-specific transactions, rate of growth, and firm size. In simplest terms, manufacturing is an "old" sector and services "new." Markets for goods are well established, compared to markets for specialized services. In most cases, pools of trained labor for manufacturing processes already exist; this is true for a smaller portion of services activity. For these and other reasons, it should be no surprise to find significant *measured* productivity differentials between manufacturing and services, even as these sectors are conventionally defined (recall that many services are performed *within* manufacturing). We should also expect to see the productivity gap between manufacturing and services gradually close as services industries "mature"; that is, as they (and other organizations) create pools of appropriate resources, specialize, apply new technologies, expand firm sizes, and exploit economies of scale — what Levitt calls "industrialization of service," but construed here somewhat more broadly.

The Treadway model is not restricted to "pure" services activities, such as internal training of a firm's workforce. It also pertains to services to goods; e.g., production workers building their own machinery. At an earlier stage of development, when manufacturing was the young, leading sector, such activities were more the rule than the exception. Thus, one would expect the productivity of pre-1890 manufacturing to be underestimated, too. In some "young" new technology industries even now, in-house development and construction of machinery are very important, as indicated above by the examples of IBM and the new semiconductor firms. The productivity problem is attributed to services, primarily because services industries are "young" industries leading the growth of the economy.

Similarly, we should expect to see differentials growing *within* the services sector, to the extent that some services activities are more constrained in realizing the "industrialization" path of development than others. There is a simple but marked division within the sector itself: between producer and consumer services. The very different growth patterns of these parts of the sector were noted in earlier chapters. Due to the higher "contact costs" and other aspects of consumer services delivery noted by Levitt, it is reasonable to expect that the potential for "industrialization" will continue to be somewhat more limited in the case of consumer than producer services. One of the important aspects of development of the services economy to be explored, in fact, is the possibility of a growing division within the sector itself, similar to the dichotomy between "productive" and "nonproductive" activities posited by Baumol (1967), which heretofore has been associated simplistically with manufacturing vis-à-vis services.

This question of duality has been explored by European analysts (Gershuny 1979; Skolka 1976). Their thesis is that there will continue to be a growing productivity gap between manufactured goods and *consumer* services, and that this (plus some other factors) will lead to a greater internalization of the latter, via greater reliance on self-service, do-it-yourself, and similar activities within households. This, in turn, they surmise, will have profound implications for the nature of work, incentives, fiscal policy, and so forth. A problem with their analysis is that they fail to discriminate among types of services and pay insufficient attention to producer services. In light of our own thinking, we tentatively conclude that the simple manufacturing/services, productive/nonproductive dichotomy is no longer very relevant. A trichotomy of major productivity gaps may be arising: among manufacturing, consumer and public services (as a group), and producer and distributive services (as a group). We hypothesize that the productivity gap between producer services and manufacturing will gradually diminish and that producer services, on balance, should become more specialized for external markets. The productivity gap between manufacturing and consumer and public services will continue to increase, and consumer services, on balance, will become more internalized. The realization of these tendencies, like others we have noted, will vary by size of organization, by scale and diversity of the urban environment, and by income group, among other factors.

The duality thesis — that one can make a sharp distinction between productive and unproductive activities — also suggests another productivity measurement dilemma as the U.S.

economy is transformed. This is the distinction between consumption and production, or between consumption and investment. The ways in which these distinctions are made seem increasingly arbitrary. One aspect of the transformation is a blurring of these boundaries and a significant overlapping of categories. Much activity that goes on within households should properly be considered forms of production or investment; for instance, child-rearing, do-it-yourself construction, etc. Likewise, much on-the-job activity might properly be considered as "consumption," especially in the services sphere (c.f. Juster's "dialogue"). The overlap is also important in marketing, since many goods or services that people purchase offer joint products in terms of a mixture of consumption and production attributes. As a result, existing measures do not adequately represent the contribution to production of activities that are labelled "consumption," nor the contribution of those "production" activities that may involve forms of consumption. Explicit recognition of the latter — the satisfaction obtained from work — is a matter of increasing concern in the design of incentives and organizational arrangements to enhance productivity. Similarly, explicit recognition of the consumption and production capabilities that can be jointly provided by services innovations (or strategic combinations of goods and services) is crucial for the creation of new services markets; e.g., for the adoption of Electronic Fund Transfer Systems (EFTS).

There is also a need to distinguish "levels" from "rates" in any discussion of productivity. The Treadway model and the internal-external transformation affecting many services, noted earlier, imply that the level of productivity of services, as of any given point in time, is likely to be underestimated, whereas the rate of change is likely to be overestimated. This may appear paradoxical, but it is also consistent with the dynamic scheme outlined earlier in this volume. Productivity is the result of the interaction of several subprocesses involving varying rates of speed and lags of varying duration. It is also the result of varying gestation periods, over which stocks of various types of human and physical capital are built up at early stages of new product, firm, industry, or sectoral development. The value of these intermediate outputs is not

captured by current measures when the outputs are produced. After many years, after new markets have taken root
and after new technologies or innovations have been embodied in resources at a sufficient scale, we may observe more
rapid rises in measured productivity. These observations,
however, will simply be measuring the end result of a dynamic
process that began many years before. If, in the meantime,
some of the dynamic linkages have been constrained or some
of the resources of innovation have dried up, the country may
be facing a serious productivity lag but not know it because of
the "laggard" indicator that conventional measures provide.
This would appear to be one explanation for the belated
recognition of the productivy problem now faced by the
United States. Current measures are simply too crude to serve
as a timely guide to policy or evaluation of policy.

Bridging the Gaps Between Theory and Policy

We noted in the first section that, in a time of transition or
transformation, it is quite characteristic for policymakers and
others to view new problems through old lenses. It is also
characteristic behavior that they will seek solutions to those
problems within the context of a framework that has gradually been formulated to explain the features of a previous
stage of development. The articulation and spread of new
ways of looking at things is itself an innovation diffusion
process that takes considerable time. Even though we can now
provide only a preliminary sorting out of complex changes in
terms of "building blocks," the concept of a disequilibrium-
dynamic process is at least helpful. It helps to see the transformation in a new light, to ask more penetrating and pertinent questions, and to pinpoint areas of strategic choice. This
concluding section will point the way.

First, as a general matter, the dynamics must be viewed as
leading to a transformation of the U.S. polity and society, not
merely its "economy." The cumulative reinforcing nature of
the processes at work means that the transformation can be
slowed and perhaps deflected, but not forestalled. Any assumptions about soon attaining a new "equilibrium" or maintaining the status quo should be discounted. The transformation spells more uncertainty, not less; more competition, not

less; and the need for major strategic decisions, not merely system maintenance.

One implication is that business and other sectors of society should look more to the social and behavioral sciences to help grapple with various aspects of the transformation and their consequences. This is not self-serving. We are faced with nothing less than a new social construction of reality. There really is no choice but to direct our science, the hallmark of our civilization, to the design and adaptation of social structures and institutions.

Most large organizations should view themselves not as mere consumers, but as producers of new knowledge: active participants in the search for new remedies. This is not primarily a matter of moral exhortation; there is also a "market" for relevant information. Most businesses have not begun to view themselves as repositories of information that can assist their own strategic planning and also feed into other sectors of society. Information of the right kind, at the right time, is extremely valuable. Correspondingly, businesses and other organizations need to be conscious of their roles in the transformation, as providers of testing grounds for a variety of organizational and behavioral "experiments" that may have considerable value in a variety of settings.

Economics is far from being the only relevant discipline. Interdisciplinary approaches need to be encouraged. Big business and many other organizations have created economics departments, but this construes much too narrowly the body of social science knowledge that needs to be mobilized. Even within economics departments per se, there is a bias toward short-term forecasting, rather than any serious effort to obtain a longer-term perspective.

Second, our dynamic perspective indicates that policies to favor innovation, adaptability, and diffusion of innovations are paramount. Fortunately, this problem area has already come to the forefront of recognition. For example, the release of a national "innovation policy" by former President Carter, based on two years of work by the Domestic Policy Council, is a step in the right direction (for details see *Science,* November 13, 1979; Hill and Utterback 1979). There is insufficient recognition, however, of the intraorganization aspects of innovation. Large organizations of all kinds face the major problem of creating or maintaining an environment within their organizations where dynamic behavior can flourish and those people who best embody such behavior can be retained. A strictly hierarchical structure, in which information flows mainly downwards and through the channels of a rigid "pecking order," is not conducive to innovation or adaptation. Innovative manufacturing organizations have loosened up intraorganizational communications channels and created environments within the firm (sometimes called "skunkworks") where thinkers, designers, engineers, marketing people, and executives interact in a very dynamic, open-ended sort of way to foster new product innovations. The creation of Bell Labs by AT&T and some of the ways the Minnesota Mining & Manufacturing Corporation operates to promote innovation are pertinent cases in point.

National policy should assist the diffusion of many types of innovations. Note here the possibility that national policy (accelerated technical progress at the macro level) and firm policy (exploiting the advantage of an innovation for as long as possible) may be at odds. But a macro policy to accelerate diffusion will intensify competition and help prevent "institutional entropy" at the micro level.

Third, there is a need to revamp economic development policies at all levels, especially at the local, state, and regional levels. There, policies are still animated by an outdated mental map of the U.S. economy. The realization that we are in the midst of a major transformation, and any responses to that realization, have been extremely slow. For instance, economic development policy is still overly influenced by a crude manufacturing/services dichotomy embodied in the "economic base" approach (Bearse 1976). An even more basic problem is the fundamentally static cast of thinking on economic development. Practitioners do not understand the dynamics of economic development (Bearse and Vaughn 1980). For example, only four or five states have taken steps to foster new, technology-based enterprise (Bearse and Konopko 1979).

Fourth, there is an urgent need for policies to maintain adequately the basic infrastructure and networks that integrate our economy. This is primarily an issue of public policy, since networks financed in a semiprivate way through user charges (e.g., the telephone network) are generally well maintained (Pagano and Moore 1981). The problem is painfully apparent in the larger cities, which have been cannibalizing their basic infrastructure for decades. There are also problems in maintaining the nation's transportation network. Fiscal and budgetary procedures by governmental bodies at all levels provide perverse incentives. In time of fiscal stress, the capital budget is the first to be cut. These problems will be aggravated by continuing inflation.

More generally, human capital resources are an equally important "infrastructure"-type resource for development. In spite of a great deal of talk about "overexpansion" in higher education, policies are still needed to maintain and upgrade human resources and enhance the flexibility of their utilization. There is depreciation accounting for physical resources in the private sector; why not for human capital and why not for physical resources in the public sector?

Fifth, our perspective suggests a need to rethink micro–macro stabilization policies and their interrelationship. The increasing interaction of the large firm with all aspects of its environment can easily lead to strategic anticompetitive strategies, whereby such firms try to control this competitive environment or insulate themselves, in so far as possible, from uncertainty. Such attempts at micro-level stabilization, as Klein (1977) indicates, are fundamentally contrary to the goal of maintaining a dynamic national economy. This is especially so to the extent that large firms try to manipulate the political process to stabilize their firm or their industry. Thus, at the national level, any tendency toward policies designed to prevent the demise of firms, even very large firms, would have to be very seriously questioned (note, for example, Hinman, 1981, on the Chrysler issue). In an environment of worldwide competition, the competitiveness of the macro economy can only be maintained to the extent that the micro units are dynamic actors. This means, among other things, that business firms will need to take a more enlightened and future-oriented approach to their role in public policy formation, not merely a defensive and reactive posture. For example, the major revamping of the regulation of financial institutions that is now underway should proceed in a way that dynamic behavior on the part of these institutions is fostered, rather than serving to congeal existing structural forms and to insulate them from uncertainty.

Sixth, business firms and other organizations, especially the larger, will have to develop explicit policies regarding their "make" versus "buy" (internalize/externalize) decisions for producer services. The nature of the complementarity of these services, and their relationship to the most strategic and dynamic concerns of the firm, must be carefully assessed within the context of each organization. Failure to do this will mean foregoing certain economies and joint products, as well as opportunities to build up internally critical masses of firm-specific human capital that can provide a comparative advantage in the dynamic sense.

Seventh, there needs to be a major research effort designed to improve productivity measurement and the development of a theoretical framework for understanding the development of an advanced economy. This should include some attempts to revise our national income and product accounts wherever feasible (Myers 1980; Goldstein 1980).

Eighth, a basic ingredient to innovation and dynamic behavior in the national economy is entrepreneurship, which is a major item on the public policy agenda. Improvements in small business financing and risk sharing; reductions in transactions costs; improvements in communications, information, and tax systems; and changes in the structure of the venture capital industry will be required. Some of these issues have been addressed by the White House Conference on small business and by recent legislation.[6] This issue is particularly important for financial and related institutions. Each in its own way must recognize the problems and opportunities presented by entrepreneurship and small business. There are many opportunities to be exploited. For example, the Big 8 accounting firms are starting to market new and additional services to the small business community.

Ninth, there are implications for human resources policy. In the economic transformations that are underway, there is a likelihood of increasing stratification and decreasing mobility

in the workforce — via depreciation and obsolescence of existing skills, capital-labor substitution, deskilling of jobs, increasing routinization of some job tasks, and increasing sophistication of others. The possibility of a growing duality in the
services sector itself was noted above. When jobs are being
abolished or redefined, skills revalued, and workplaces reorganized or relocated, existing channels for occupational
mobility may be foreclosed or impeded.

There may be an increasingly serious problem of mobility
between the blue collar and white collar portions of the labor
force. It is likely that the brunt of the problem of adapting the
nation's economy to automation has not yet been felt. Given
the rapid pace of technological developments in automatic
control and robotization of manufacturing processes in recent
years, it seems that the "automation" debate of the 1960s was
somewhat premature. What really gave the debate currency at
that time was less the cost-effective nature or widespread
applicability of control systems than the postwar wave of investment in plant and equipment. Sometime in the 1980s we
will probably face a double problem of economic adjustment:
relatively low cost control systems that can be widely adopted,
and the possibility (as yet unrealized) of a new wave of investment in response to low productivity, international competition, and a variety of changes in economic policy. The
gradual, long-term diminution of production worker employment will accelerate. As a source and site of employment,
the factory is well on its way to becoming as insignificant as the
farm.

There is at least a *prima-facie* case, therefore, for much more
attention to the adjustment costs of economic transformation.
The redesign and integration of policies and programs in
several interrelated areas will be necessary; for instance, with
respect to manpower training and retraining, depreciation,
schedules, taxation, plant shutdowns, migration, and relocation. One must ask again: Since it is appropriate to account for
the depreciation and obsolescence of physical capital, why not
human capital, too?

Finally, with respect to education, one cannot help but be
struck by the increasingly archaic cast of the services
enterprise for learning and teaching called the university. In

attempting to dissect the transformation of the U.S. economy, it has been both desirable and necessary to turn to a variety of fields. There is no significant policy issue one can name that does not require interdisciplinary attention. Yet academia is a fractioned enterprise, increasingly characterized by specializations and arcane tongues. The concept of "transformation" cannot be articulated within any one field. The lack of serious interdisciplinary work in academic settings is most troublesome in the social sciences, which are most directly implicated in policy design and implementation.[7] What little progress is being made in interdisciplinary work is mainly in nonacademic settings — in think tanks, engineering consulting firms, and government agencies. Why? Perhaps Herbert Simon's basis hypothesis is a propos: "Behavior is contingent upon the structure of the environment." (There is also a cynic's version called "Miles Law" in public administration: "How one thinks depends on where one sits.") The structure of the academic environment (including its incentives) is not at all conducive to interdisciplinary projects; therefore, a large part of that environment's output is not "rational" in the sense of being able to diagnose the economy's transformation or to prescribe adequate policies for its management. A major restructuring of the research enterprise in academia is called for if interdisciplinary studies are to take root and begin to generate the new knowledge we need.

Tenth, there will have to be a wholesale, systematic reformulation of public policy in this era of transformation. Prevailing views concerning the relative roles of government and private enterprise are much too narrow. Many emerging markets are neither conventionally "private" nor "public" but an admixture. There are, therefore, increasingly subtle policy choices to be made since the mode of provision of various services is "up for grabs" with respect to legal forms of organization, incentives, financing, and other arrangements. The role of government in the U.S. economy has never been as narrow as economic theorists conceived it to be (Witte 1957), and in fact may have to be broadened in future if the adjustment costs of transformation are to be borne equitably and efficiently. Similarly, the role of private business, especially large corporations, is increasingly public in nature. One can easily envisage a shuffling and shifting of certain functions between sectors: government carrying out certain functions formerly thought to be the exclusive franchise of private business, and private business carrying out certain functions that were formerly thought to be peculiar to government. The narrowly construed role of government as regulator and government as employer-of-last resort will to some extent have to be supplemented by government as investor, government as producer, government as risk-taker, and government as entrepreneur (cf., Bearse 1976). On their part, the more sophisticated and alert portions of the private sector will find that there are many public markets for them to enter. It is already obvious, as in areas of environmental protection and safety, that the interaction of public and private will continue to create new markets, following the old adage that one man's problem is another's opportunity.

A corollary is that there will be a continued need in both sectors to experiment with organizational forms that might incorporate the best features of public and private enterprise. The rapid growth of private, nonprofit forms is itself witness to the growing gray area between public and private.

The financial sector, especially, is one area where the dynamic tension between public and private is apparent, and where one can look for some of the above tendencies to work themselves out. Recent debates over the Chrysler bail-out, tax expenditures, the implementation of the Community Reinvestment Act, and federal credit policies are not merely episodic, they are symptomatic (for several examples of public-private institutional innovation in the field of development finance, see Bearse 1981).

Concluding Remarks

This chapter has attempted to provide a conceptual synthesis, an integrated view at a mid-range of discourse, of the dynamic process by which the U.S. economy is being transformed. It is a first attempt at a very difficult task of reconceptualization that should proceed from many contributions and many levels, from the broad-brush descriptive to the rigorous mathematical, and from many fields of inquiry. If some of the "building blocks" and their interconnections seem oversimplified, it is for reasons of space and understanding, reflecting a deliberate attempt at simplification to highlight only the most important forces and linkages. Each of the building blocks will need to be elaborated so that more specific statements can be set forth, rigorously and in a way that enables their evaluation against available data. Ultimately, a comprehensive theoretical structure will have to be erected using the (refined) building blocks as modules. As indicated above, the delineation of hypothetical cause and effect relationships by way of path diagrams is a useful way to begin. Proceeding further, to build and test dynamic models involving complex lead/lag relationships is an arduous undertaking involving many years of work.

If there is a single concept that has proved useful in grappling with transformation as a dynamic process, it is the concept of "diffusion." We observe exponential and combinatorial increases in the body of knowledge of the physical world, in computing power, and in the speed and connectivity of communications networks. In the first instance, however, these developments mainly imply an increase in the *potential variety* of innovations and an increase in the *potential speed* by which innovations can filter through the economy. These potentials may or may not be realized, or may be realized at greater or lesser speeds, depending on a variety of structural factors. The fact that an advanced industrial economy possesses a sophisticated infrastructure, highly articulated networks, a well-developed system of cities, rich human capital resources, etc., does not mean that such an economy is necessarily more dynamic or adaptive.

The adaptability and flexibility of basic socio-economic structures is at issue — their ability to adopt, adapt, and rapidly exploit potential innovations.

Potential innovations arise at many levels. In the midst of a major transformation from one stage of development to another, what is fundamentally at issue is the ability of the major structures themselves to be transformed.

What are "basic structures?" The organization of work, the spatial organization of the economy, the political and governmental system, institutional arrangements for the generation and transmission of knowledge, and the ideological framework that conditions how people perceive these other structures and the potential for changing them.

If the institutional framework of an advanced economy is in some sense dominated by large bureaucratic structures, both public and private, then the adaptability of that economy in an era of transformation is problematic; that is, an issue to be confronted. One should anticipate the possibility that the dynamic process outlined above could go another way — from a process of positive reinforcement to one of negative reinforcement; from one of growth to one of stagnation or decline. Again, one of the most central and symptomatic concerns is productivity, since it is not just the end product of a dynamic process of development; it is a basic factor in that process.

The adaptability of systems is somewhat contingent upon the existence of slack or surplus resources. If some of the basic, positive forces in the innovation-diffusion process outlined earlier are weakened, so that growth of productivity diminishes, then whatever exists in the way of slack or surplus to help support innovative activity is likely to be used up. Thus, the ability of the economic system to innovate and adapt basic structures to new circumstances may be further diminshed. If, as suggested above, the decline is not taken into account for several years, several more years pass before ameliorative measures are enacted, and several more again before they have any palpable effect, an advanced economy can enter into a long period of stagnation or decline before the forces of decline are arrested.

Thus, this attempt to conceptualize the transformation of the U.S. economy in a way that is relevant to policy concerns points to an evaluation of the adaptability of basic structures as the foremost concern of both analysis and policy. This conclusion is highlighted by a series of questions to be addressed in future work.

A. Is the spatial organization of the economy which has evolved in the postwar period a suitable matrix for a developing services economy?

B. Are hierarchical structures of production inherited from the manufacturing era adaptable to requirements of innovation, flexibility, increased productivity and the need to distribute equitably the fruits of technical progress?

C. What changes are required in institutional arrangements to facilitate the generation, transmission, and application of knowledge?

D. What aspects of the political system, government, and ideology impede the adoption of policies that are necessitated by the transformation?

A fundamental problem associated with the last question is the pervasive short-term time horizon of the governmental and political parts of our economic system. The transition and transformation we have been describing in this volume has been going on for several decades and will likely continue over the remainder of this century. The dynamic, developmental processes we have sketched to try to elucidate the transforma-ion are long term in nature. The productivity problem, in particular, has been arising over the past 15 to 18 years and will take at least a decade to resolve. Whether our political and governmental institutions can help complete the socio-economic transition successfully remains to be seen.

Notes

[1]The tendency for large R&D facilities to locate "off center" is important to note, however. Cf. Chapter 5 and Dunn, (1980).

[2]This was recognized by Thompson (1965) in his framework for urban development and a stylistic example of such a process is sketched below in the discussion of productivity.

[3]Thurow's (1975) and Stiglitz's (1978) analysis of labor and capital markets are at least consistent with this statement, although they might not subscribe to this catholic interpretation.

[4]A simple but quite satisfactory example is Baumol's (1980) attempt to construct an "operational model of entrepreneurship." This could be incorporated into the dynamic framework sketched in this section.

[5]A seeming exception to this is the internalization of producer services by large corporate units. The many reasons why producer services may continue to be internalized, even though the services may no longer be "new" services, were outlined earlier in Chapter 3. Yet, as indicated there, continued internalization is not inconsistent with the simultaneous development of an external services market.

[6]For example, the Small Business Investment Incentive Act of 1980.

[7]Nevertheless, the fruitfulness of an interdisciplinary approach to conventional economic issues is illustrated by a few choice examples. See, for example, two recent works on consumption — one by Scitovsky (1976), which integrates insights from economics and psychology, and another by Douglas (1980), which integrates insights from economics and anthropology.

Appendix Table A.1 Analysis of Employment Change by Occupation for Services and Nonservices, 1960 to 1967 and 1970 to 1976

Occupation	1960 to 1967					1970 to 1976				
	Gain at national growth rate	"Expected" additional gain (loss) due to industry growth	"Shift": Additional gain (loss)	Net change	Employment share (%)	Gain at national growth rate	"Expected" additional gain (loss) due to industry growth	"Shift": Additional gain (loss)	Net change	Employment share (%)
	Service industries					*Service industries*				
Total	4,999,618	2,487,327	0	7,486,945	100.00	5,657,905	3,000,700	0	8,179,655	100.00
Professional	530,997	1,266,634	401,441	2,199,072	12.16	695,731	795,158	-311,234	1,179,655	12.49
Technical	277,561	429,048	74,176	780,735	6.23	401,454	352,443	504,245	1,258,142	8.20
Manager	746,797	75,779	-354,759	467,817	13.56	685,038	275,915	483,923	1,444,876	12.79
Office clerical	370,187	321,372	86,354	605,205	8.18	609,690	445,487	-87,820	967,857	10.84
Nonoffice clerical	590,645	318,081	171,816	1,080,542	12.72	600,319	197,297	30,868	828,484	10.46
Sales workers	487,156	-87,378	-137,059	262,719	8.74	498,811	102,894	126,106	475,599	8.32
Craft workers	376,195	-78,890	159,925	457,230	7.42	419,285	-52,505	153,546	520,326	7.20
Operatives	471,484	-103,058	68,527	436,953	8.95	448,504	-109,545	-75,433	263,526	7.20
Service workers	944,179	393,117	-242,453	1,094,843	18.37	1,064,426	1,030,356	-631,501	1,463,281	18.53
Laborers	204,417	-47,378	-55,260	101,779	3.67	234,647	-36,800	59,012	256,859	3.97
Services					61.52					67.46
	Nonservice industries					*Nonservice industries*				
Total	3,594,333	-2,487,327	0	1,107,006	100.00	3,182,405	-3,000,700	0	181,705	100.00
Professional	126,060	-13,425	112,772	225,407	4.16	127,167	-124,474	82,958	85,651	4.27
Technical	98,048	-14,365	29,313	112,996	3.02	120,491	-127,728	111,360	104,123	4.13
Manager	1,001,309	-2,250,237	-143,063	-1,391,991	21.92	504,596	-468,825	97,699	133,470	16.23
Office clerical	127,358	-6,225	42,415	163,548	3.98	175,791	-177,426	-22,016	-23,651	5.41
Nonoffice clerical	187,224	6,019	4,258	197,501	5.70	135,748	-146,610	-47,116	-57,978	4.03
Sales workers	64,713	4,073	-37,388	31,398	1.84	56,577	-64,529	15,268	7,316	1.79
Craft workers	624,515	-120,232	-510	503,773	18.46	636,185	-444,326	73,593	265,452	20.80
Operatives	1,058,120	-8,400	379,850	1,429,580	33.29	1,030,096	-1,112,666	-118,849	-201,419	31.45
Service workers	47,201	-2,632	-74,419	-29,850	1.16	53,698	-56,979	-65,087	-68,368	1.43
Laborers	259,785	-81,903	-313,238	-135,356	6.47	342,056	-277,137	-127,810	-62,891	10.46
Nonservices					38.48					32.54

Source: U.S. Bureau of Labor Statistics, *Tomorrow's Manpower Needs, Industry-Occupational Matrix*, Microdata, 1960, 1967, 1970 and 1976.

Appendix Table A.2 140 Largest SMSAs Clustered in Eleven Type Groups, 1976

National nodal	SMSA size	Regional nodal	SMSA size	Subregional nodal	SMSA size	Functional nodal	SMSA size	Government (& Education)	SMSA size	Education and Manufacturing	SMSA size
1 New York	1	4 Philadelphia	1	41 Memphis	3	5 Detroit	1	8 Washington, DC	1	54 New Haven	3
2 Los Angeles	1	6 Boston	1	45 Salt Lake City	3	13 Pittsburgh	1	39 Sacramento	3	64 Springfield	3
3 Chicago	1	10 Dallas	1	52 Nashville	3	16 Newark	1	48 Albany	3	90 Tacoma	4
7 San Francisco	1	11 Houston	1	53 Oklahoma City	3	24 Milwaukee	2	77 Raleigh–Durham	4	130 South Bend	4
		12 St. Louis	1	56 Jacksonville	3	31 San Jose	2	81 Fresno	4	140 Ann Arbor	4
		14 Baltimore	1	58 Syracuse	3	36 Hartford	2	82 Austin	4		
		15 Minneapolis	1	65 Richmond	3	38 Rochester	3	84 Lansing	4		
		17 Cleveland	1	66 Charlotte	3	40 Louisville	3	85 Oxnard–Ventura	4		
		18 Atlanta	2	69 Omaha	3	44 Dayton	3	88 Harrisburg	4		
		21 Miami	2	101 Little Rock	4	47 Bridgeport	3	89 Baton Rouge	4		
		22 Denver	2	110 Des Moines	4	50 Toledo	3	99 Columbia, SC	4		
		23 Seattle	2	114 Spokane	4	51 Greensboro	3	111 Utica	4		
		26 Cincinnati	2	120 Jackson MS	4	57 Akron	3	112 Trenton	4		
		28 Kansas City	2			62 Allentown	3	113 Madison	4		
		30 Phoenix	2			63 Tulsa	3	117 Stockton	4		
		32 Indianapolis	2			67 New Brunswick	3				
		33 New Orleans	2			70 Jersey City	3				
		34 Portland	2			75 Wilmington	3				
		35 Columbus	2			78 Paterson	4				
						86 Knoxville	4				
						96 Wichita	4				
						100 Fort Wayne	4				
						103 Peoria	4				
						137 Kalamazoo	4				

Residential	SMSA size
9 Nassau	1
19 Anaheim	2
76 Long Branch	3

Resort — Retirement	SMSA size
25 Tampa	2
29 Riverside	2
43 Ft. Lauderdale	3
55 Honolulu	3
68 Orlando	3
79 West Palm Beach	4
95 Albuquerque	4
108 Las Vegas	4
122 Santa Barbara	4

Manufacturing	SMSA size
27 Buffalo	2
42 Providence	3
46 Birmingham	3
59 Worcester	3
60 Gary	3
61 N.E. Pennsylvania	3
71 Grand Rapids	3
72 Youngstown	3
73 Greenville	3
74 Flint	3
80 New Bedford	4
91 Mobile	4
92 Canton	4
93 Johnson City	4
94 Chattanooga	4
98 Davenport	4
104 Beaumont	4
106 Shreveport	4
107 York	4
109 Lancaster	4
115 Binghamton	4
116 Reading	4
119 Huntington	4
121 Lexington	4
124 Evansville	4
125 Appleton	4
131 Erie	4
134 Rockford	4
136 Lorain	4

Industrial and military	SMSA size
20 San Diego	2
37 San Antonio	3
49 Norfolk	3
87 El Paso	4
97 Charleston, SC	4
102 Newport News	4
123 Huntsville	4
126 Augusta	4
127 Vallejo	4
128 Colorado Springs	4
132 Pensacola	4
133 Salinas	4

Mining (& Manufacturing)	SMSA size
83 Tucson	4
105 Bakersfield	4
118 Corpus Christi	4
129 Lakeland	4
135 Johnstown, PA	4
138 Duluth	4
139 Charleston, WV	4

Note: Number preceding name of SMSA indicates 1976 population size rank. Number following name of SMSA indicates population size group (see text).

Source: T. Novelle and T. Stanback, *Economic Transformations in American Cities,* 1981.

Bibliography

Abramovitz, Moses. "Manpower, Capital and Technology." In *Human Resources and Economic Welfare, Essays in Honor of Eli Ginzberg*, edited by Ivar Berg. New York: Columbia University Press, 1972.

Baumol, William. "The Macroeconomics of Unbalanced Growth," *American Economic Review*, 1967.

———"Towards Operational Models of Entrepeneurship," Price Institute for Entrepeneurial Studies. New York University, 1980.

Bearse, Peter J. "Government as Innovator: A New Paradigm for State Economic Development Policy." *New England Journal of Business and Economics*, Spring 1976.

———"On the Intra-Regional Diffusion of Business Services Activity." *Regional Studies*, vol. 12 #5, 1978.

———*Mobilizing Capital. Program Innovation and the Changing Public-Private Interface in Development Finance*. New York: Elsvier North Holland, Forthcoming 1981.

Bearse, Peter J., and D. Konopko. "A Comparative Analysis of State Programs to Assist New Technology Based Enterprise." *New England Journal of Business and Economics*, Spring 1979.

Bearse, Peter J., and Roger Vaughn. *Federal Economic Development Strategy: a Framework for Design and Evaluation* Washington, D.C.: National Commission for Employment Policy, October 1980.

Becker, Gary. "Dialogue on the Service Economy." In *Abstracts of Dialogues on the Service Economy*. New York: Conservation of Human Resources, 1980.

Bloch, Ernest. "Faculty Underemployment." *Report 77-16*, Graduate School of Business Administration, New York University, April 1977.

Caves, Richard E. "Industrial Organization, Corporate Strategy, and Structure." *Journal of Economic Literature* 28, March 1980, pp. 64–92.

Chandler, Alfred. *The Visible Hand: The Managerial Revolution in American Business*. Cambridge, Mass.: Harvard University Press, 1977.

Cohen, Robert. *The Internationalization of Capital and U.S. Cities*, Ph.D. dissertation, New School for Social Research, 1979.

Cohen, Robert et al. *The Transformation of the Corporation: Hypotheses and Preliminary Findings.* New York: Conservation of Human Resources 1980.

Conservation of Human Resources. *The Corporate Headquarters Complex in New York City.* New York: Conservation of Human Resources, 1977.

————. *Abstracts of Dialogues on the Service Economy.* New York: Conservation of Human Resources, 1980. Mimeograph.

Csikszentmihalyi, Mihaily. *Beyond Boredom and Anxiety.* San Francisco: Jossey Bass, 1975.

Davies, R. *The Diffusion of Process Innovations.* New York: Cambridge University Press, 1979.

Denison, Edward. *Accounting for Slower Economic Growth: The U.S. in the 1970s.* Washington, D.C.: Brookings Institution, 1979.

Douglas, Mary. *The World of Goods.* New York: Basic Books, 1980.

Duncan, Beverly,and Stanley Lieberson. *Metropolis and Region in Transition.* Beverly Hills, California: Sage Publications, 1970.

Dunn, Edgar S. Jr. *The Development of the U.S. Urban System,* vol. 1. Baltimore: The Johns Hopkins University Press, 1980.

Freedman, Marcia. *Labor Markets: Segments and Shelters.* Montclair, N.J.: Allanheld, Osmun & Co., 1976.

————. *The Transformation of the U.S. Labor Force* (forthcoming).

Fuchs, Victor. *The Services Economy.* New York: National Bureau of Economic Research and Columbia University Press, 1968.

————. "The Service Industries and U.S. Economic Growth since World War II." *Working Paper #211,* National Bureau of Economic Research, Center for Economic Analysis of Human Behavior and Social Institutions, Standford: November, 1977.

————. "Dialogue on the Service Economy." In *Abstracts of Dialogues on the Service Economy.* New York: Conservation of Human Resources, 1980.

Gans, Herbert. *Popular Culture and High Culture.* New York: Basic Books, 1975.

Georgescu-Roegen, Nicholas. *The Entropy Law and the Economic Process.* Cambridge, Mass.: Harvard University Press, 1972.

Gershuny, J.I. and R.E. Pahl. "Towards An Alternative Society." Paper read at *Social Science Research Council Workshop on Unemployment and Employment,* London, Sept. 28, 1979.

Goldstein, Harold. "Recent Structural Changes in Employment in the United States." Paper commissioned by Conservation of Human Resources, New York, February, 1980.

Gordon, David M. "Capitalist Development and the History of American Cities." In William K. Tabb and Larry Sawers, *Marxism and the Metropolis.* New York: Oxford University Press, 1978.

Greenfield, Harry I. *Manpower and the Growth of Producer Services.* New York: Columbia University Press, 1966.

Grilisches, Zvi. "Issues in Assessing the Contribution of Research and Development to Productivity Growth." *Bell Journal of Economics,* 1979, p. 92.

Harrison, Bennett, and Edward Hill. "The Changing Structure of Jobs in Older and Younger Cities." In Benjamin Chinitz, *Central City Economic Development.* Cambridge, Mass.: Abt Books, 1979.

Hill, Christopher, and James Utterback. *Technical Innovation for a Dynamic Economy.* New York: Pergamon Press, 1979.

Hinman, Keith. "Lemon Capitalism? An Analysis of the Chrysler Bail-Out." In Peter J. Bearse op. cit., 1981.

Juster, Thomas. "Dialogue on the Service Economy." In *Abstracts of Dialogues on the Service Economy.* New York: Conservation of Human Resources, 1980.

Karasek, Robert A. "Job Demands, Job Decision Latitude and Mental Strain: Implications for Job Redesign." *Administration Science Quarterly* 4, (June 1979).

————"A Theory of Services in the Consumer Economy." Paper commissioned by Conservation of Human Resources, New York, 1980a.

————"New Value Economics." *Working paper,* Department of Industrial Engineering and Operations Research. New York: Columbia University, 1980b.

————"Job Socialization and Job Strain: The Implication for Two Related Mechanisms for Job Redesign." In B. Jordell and G. Johannson, ed., *Man and Working Life, Social Science Contributions to Work Reform.* London: John Wiley, 1980c.

Klein, Burton. *Dynamic Economics.* Cambridge, Mass.: Harvard University Press, 1977.

Klein, Burton H. "Hidden–foot Feedback: Wellspring of Economic Utility." *Technology Review,* October 1980, p. 46.

Knight, Richard. *The Cleveland Economy in Transition: Implications for the Future.* Report to Study Participants. Cleveland: Cleveland State University, July 1977.

Kuznets, Simon. "Dialogue on the Service Economy." In *Abstracts of Dialogues on the Service Economy.* New York: Conservation of Human Resources, 1980.

Lampard, Eric. "The History of Cities in the Economically Advanced Areas." *Economic Development and Cultural Change,* vol. 3, p. 573, 1955.

Lancaster, Kelvin. *Variety, Equity and Efficiency: Product Variety in An Industrial Society.* New York: Columbia University Press, 1979.

Lebergott, Stanley. *The American Economy: Income, Wealth and Want.* Princeton, New Jersey: Princeton University Press, 1967.

Levitt, Theodore. "The Industrialization of Service." *Harvard Business Review,* September 1976.

Linder, Steffan. *The Harried Leisure Class.* New York: Columbia University Press, 1970.

Malecki, Edward J. "Locational Trends in R&D by Large U.S. Corporations, 1965–1977." *Economic Geography,* 1979.

Mansfield, Edwin. "Technical Change in the Rate of Imitation." *Econometrica,* 1961.

Maruyama, M. "The Second Cybernetics: Deviation Amplifying Mutual Causal Processes." *American Scientist,* vol. # 51, 1963, p. 164.

Maslow, Abraham H. *Toward a Psychology of Being.* New York: Van Nostrand, Rheinhold, 1968.

Meier, Richard. *A Communications Theory of Urban Growth.* Cambridge, Mass.: M.I.T. Press, 1962.

Mollenkopf, John H. "Paths Toward the Post Industrial Service City: The Northeast and the Southwest." Working Paper, Program on Urban Studies. Stanford University, 1979.

Myers, John. "GNP: Perspectives on Services." Paper prepared for the Conservation of Human Resources, New York, March 1980.

Noyelle, Thierry J., and Thomas M. Stanback, Jr. *Economic Transformation in American Cities.* New York: Conservation of Human Resources. Forthcoming.

Pagano, Michael, and Richard Moore. "Emerging Issues in Financing Basic Infrastructure." In Peter J. Bearse, op. cit., 1981.

Penrose, Edith. *The Growth of the Firm.* London: John Wiley, 1959.

Perry, David C., and Alfred J. Watkins. *The Rise of the Sunbelt Cities.* Beverly Hills, California: Sage Publications, 1977.

Pred, Allan. "The Location of High Value-Added Manufacturing." *Economic Geography* 108 (1965):41.

―――.*The Spatial Dynamics of U.S. Urban Industrial Growth, 1800 – 1914.* Cambridge, Mass.: M.I.T. Press, 1966.

―――.*City-Systems in Advanced Economies.* New York: John Wiley & Sons, 1977.

Sanuki, Toshio. "The City in Informational Society." *Area Development in Japan,* volume #3. Tokyo: 1970. p. 9.

Scitovsky, Tibor. *The Joyless Economy.* London: Oxford University Press, 1976.

Simon, Herbert. *Models of Man.* London: John Wiley, 1957.

―――."On Parsimonious Explanations of Production Relations." *Scandinavian Journal of Economics,* 1979.

Singlemann, Joachim. *From Agriculture to Services.* Beverly Hills, California: Sage Publications, 1978.

Skolka, J.V. "Long-term Effects of Unbalanced Labour Productivity Growth: On the Way to a Self-Service Society." In *Private and Enlarged Consumption: Essays in Methodology and Empirical Analysis,* L. Solavi and J.R. duPasqueri, eds. New York: North Holland, 1976.

Stanback, Thomas M. Jr. *Understanding the Service Economy: Employment, Productivity, Location.* Baltimore: Johns Hopkins University Press, 1979.

Stanback, Thomas M. Jr., and Richard V. Knight. *The Metropolitan Economy.* New York: Columbia University Press, 1970.

Stanback, Thomas M. Jr., and Thierry J. Noyelle. *Metropolitan Labor Markets in Transition: A Study of Seven SMSAs.* Commissioned by the U.S. Department of Labor. New York: Conservation of Human Resources, April 1981.

Starr, Martin K. "Productivity and Production Management." *Working paper* New York: Columbia University, Graduate School of Business, 1979.

Sternlieb, George, and James W. Hughes, eds. *Post Industrial America: Metropolitan Decline and Inter-Regional Job Shifts.* New Brunswick, N.J.: The Center for Urban Policy Research, 1975.

Stigler, George. "The Division of Labor Is Limited by the Extent of the Market." *Journal of Political Economy* 59 (June 1951): 185.

―――. *Trends in Employment in the Service Industries.* Princeton, New Jersey: Princeton University Press, 1956.

Stiglitz, Joseph. "Information and Economic Analysis." Stanford Institute for Mathematical Studies and the Social Sciences, *Reprint #201.* Stanford University, 1978.

Sylos-Labini, P. *Oligopoly and Technical Progress.* Cambridge: Harvard University Press, 1957.

Thompson, Wilbur. *Preface to Urban Economics.* Baltimore: The Johns Hopkins University Press, 1965.

Thurow, Lester. *Generating Inequality.* New York: Basic Books, 1975.

Toffler, Alvin. *Future Shock.* New York: Bantam Books, 1970.

Treadway, Arthur. "What is Output?" In *Production and Productivity in the*

Service Industries, V. Fuchs, ed. National Bureau of Economic Research, Stanford, 1968.

U.S. Bureau of Labor Statistics. *Consumer Expenditure Survey: Interview Survey, 1972 – 1973.* Washington, D.C.: U.S. Department of Labor, 1978.

U.S. Department of Housing. *The President's National Urban Policy Report.* Washington, D.C.: U.S. Government Printing Office, 1980.

Watkins, Alfred J. *The Practice of Urban Economics.* Beverly Hills, California: Sage Publications, 1980.

Williamson, Oliver. "Transaction Costs Economics: The Governance of Contractual Relations." *Journal of Law and Economics,* March 1980.

Witte, Edwin. "Economics and Public Policy." *American Economic Review,* March 1957.

Newspaper Articles

Business Week, September 18, 1978. "Texas Instruments Shows U.S. Business How to Survive in the 1980s."

New York Times, March 16, 1980. "Suburbia: End of the Golden Age," by William Severini Kowinski.

New York Times, March 23, 1980. "Urban Centers' Population Drift Creating A Countryside Harvest."

Science, November 19, 1979.

Wall Street Journal, December 6, 1979.

Index

The Authors

Thomas M. Stanback, Jr. teaches economics at New York University and is Senior Research Associate at the Conservation of Human Resources Project, Columbia University. He is the author of *Understanding the Service Economy* and coauthor of *The Metropolitan Economy: The Process of Employment Expansion* and of *Suburbanization and the City*.

Peter J. Bearse is Director of Economic Development for the Corporation for Public/Private Ventures in Philadelphia. He has worked and written extensively in the areas of urban, state, and regional economic problems and policies. He is the editor of *Mobilizing Capital: Probram Innovation and the Changing Public/Private Interface in Development Finance*.

Thierry J. Noyelle is Research Associate at the Conservation of Human Resources Project, Columbia University. He has written in the areas of urban and regional development, economic planning, and labor market segmentation.

Robert A. Karasek is Assistant Professor of Industrial Engineering and Operations Research at Columbia University. He has worked and written in the areas of work-related mental and physical stress, job redesign, and productivity measurement. He is currently investigating theories of consumption, nonmarket production, and human capital development.